This Book Presented by

SHMUEL GREENBAUM

A Daily Dose of Kindness

A Daily Dose of Kindness

STORIES FROM THE HEART

A Response to Terror

BOOK ONE:
In Love with Israel

Shmuel Greenbaum

Partners in Kindness, Inc.
www.PartnersInKindness.org

Published by
Partners In Kindness, Inc.
545 Eighth Avenue, Suite 401
New York, NY 10018

www.PartnersInKindness.org

For quickest response please contact us by e-mail at:
info@PartnersInKindness.org

ISBN: 978-0-578-00203-3

Library of Congress Control Number: 2009900093

First Edition

This book is available at quantity discounts for bulk purchase.

For information, visit www.PartnersInKindness.org or e-mail
info@PartnersInKindness.org

10 9 8 7 6 5 4 3 2 1

Printed in the United States of America

Thank You

This book would not be possible without the hundreds of people who contributed stories, volunteered their time and provided financial support. A special section contains all the sponsor dedications. Thank you to everyone who helped.

– Shmuel Greenbaum

Contents

Foreword

Life, when all is said and done, is about the choices we make. For all our formidable power, we humans cannot control all the events in this universe. Nor can we predict if or when we will be confronted by tragedy, loss or misfortune. But—how we react to the challenges thrown our way, and what we do in the face of adversity is indeed our decision, our choice. And it is precisely how we respond to life's unpleasant surprises that will shape who we are, and afford us the opportunity to impact other lives.

A Daily Dose of Kindness is a book born out of a senseless tragedy, a response of good in the face of overwhelming evil. We never know how many lives are touched and often changed by something good.

In a world torn by war and hatred, *A Daily Dose of Kindness* is a testament to the goodwill that exists in the hearts of so many people who do acts of kindness for others without consideration of race or religion. These testimonies come from all kinds of people and from all over the world.

This book represents the choice of a grief-stricken man who chose to rise above his loss by encouraging acts of kindness rather than succumbing to bitterness and despair. It is a fitting memorial to Shoshana Greenbaum, may her memory inspire us all to act with kindness. Shoshana's violent death became the catalyst for an enterprise that has not only brightened the days of many people, but has also changed their lives.

Reading stories from *A Daily Dose of Kindness* about the goodness of friend to friend, family to family, and stranger to stranger can help to bridge the gaps between cultures and religions; it can transform a world filled with callousness and conceit into a world of caring; it can turn strangers into friends.

An incident that illustrates this point happened to me many years ago. When I decided to go to medical school I was married with two children and a third on the way. I held a low-paying position as an assistant rabbi and my father helped support me and my family.

The tuition for medical school was formidable but I was able to manage for a while, using donations from my congregation and some loans. But by the middle of my third year, I was in debt up to my ears and unable to go on. I wrote to foundations that gave scholarships to medical students, but I was turned down. What to do?

I usually called home during the day to see how my wife was feeling and one day she said, "What would you do if you had four thousand dollars?"

"I'd travel around the world." Can't she see I'm busy, I said to myself. "I have no time for daydreaming," is what I said aloud.

"This is not a daydream. There is a check for four thousand dollars on its way to you."

"Did you forge it?"

"No, Danny Thomas is giving you four thousand dollars."

I had no idea who Danny Thomas was and wondered if perhaps my wife's pregnancy was making her a little strange. But after we'd gone back and forth about this check, she read to me the following story out of the Chicago Sun-Times.

At a meeting with officials from Marquette University, the officials told Danny Thomas about the plight of a young rabbi who was having a difficult time financing his education. "How much does the rabbi need?" Danny Thomas asked. "About four thousand dollars," the Marquette officials said. "Tell your rabbi he's got it." Like it happened all the time, I thought. But sure enough several days later I received a call from Danny Thomas who affirmed that the money was coming in a few days.

For the rest of Danny Thomas's life, we were in touch. I have no idea what Danny received spiritually from his generosity to strangers. I do know that I received a medical degree as well as confirmation of my belief and pride in humankind.

One material return Danny Thomas received came about many years later and I am forever grateful for having been a part of it.

Danny traveled around the country raising money for the hospital he had built that specialized in leukemia, the Shrine of St. Jude. He came to Milwaukee to raise money and I contacted people on his behalf asking that they attend a fund-raising dinner.

That evening I was given the opportunity to make a presentation to Danny Thomas of the pledges we had raised for the charity which meant so much to him. At this time I shared with everyone what Danny had done for me. I was embarrassed by my tearfulness and avoided looking out at the group. But finally as I presented Danny with a gift, I had to look up and that's when I found many of those in the room weeping the same tears of gratitude and admiration for this great, kind man. I also gave him a beautiful volume of the Bible with a silver filigree cover inscribed with this verse from Micah: "For what does the Lord God ask of you, but to act with kindness, do justice and walk humbly with your God."

Acts of kindness not only bind but also break through barriers, bringing people together as the brothers they should be. Who would think of a less likely combination: a Lebanese Christian and a Chassidic rabbi?

Abraham Twerski, M.D.

Introduction

This book is an outgrowth of the life and tragic murder of my wife Shoshana. Shoshana's goal in life was to reach out with her love to each and every soul she touched; to infuse each one with self esteem; to comfort each one in their sadness; and to raise each one to their highest potential.

Her life was dedicated to truth and kindness. She inspired men and women of all religions with her ways. She was the perfect role model for the children she taught. Shoshana dedicated her life to elevating each and every one of the hundreds of children she taught to become just like she was. In the process she also inspired their parents and all the others she met wherever she went.

Shoshana taught us that our sensitivity and caring for others must extend much further than to merely our relatives. Shoshana was sensitive to the children who lost parents or had other challenges at home. She would go out of her way never to say anything which could make them feel uncomfortable. She would always try to give them strength and comfort them. She engrained her strength in them and made them truly believe that, as she used to tell them, "There is good in every bad."

Husbands and wives not only share a common mission in

life but they share a soul. And so, I know that whatever I have done after Shoshana's death is what we would have done together were she alive.

How It All Began

The year 2001 started out to be wonderful. In January, we had been married just under a year when my wife and I left New York City to move into our new home in the suburbs. A few months later, we were overjoyed to find out that Shoshana was pregnant with our first child.

That summer was the highlight of our marriage. Shoshana had won a full scholarship to graduate school which included six weeks of study in Israel. We spent four of those weeks together, enjoying every minute, until our joy came to a crashing halt on August 9, 2001. My wife and unborn child were murdered by a terrorist bomber in a Jerusalem restaurant.

One month later, nearly 3,000 people were killed by terrorists in New York, Pennsylvania and Washington, D.C. The world was in shock and fear. The feeling of terror was paralyzing. It made us feel helpless and alone.

What pulled me through this tragedy was the kindness of friends and relatives and most importantly, the kindness of strangers who no longer wanted to be strangers, but only wanted to open up their hearts to do whatever they could to help.

How could I feel helpless when I saw everyone helping? I wanted to be like them and help others, too. How could I feel alone when so many people who hardly knew me showed how much they cared?

Strangers performed extraordinary acts of kindness for others after September 11. They traveled great distances and risked their lives to search through the wreckage; they donated money and blood; they prayed for the missing and for their own uncertain futures.

The more people realized that others were helping, the more they themselves wanted to help. In an amazing turn of events, powerful negative emotional forces of hatred were channeled into positive emotional forces of kindness. Imagine how much better the world would be if this powerful desire to help could be harnessed.

Partners in Kindness

On January 1, 2002, four months after my wife's murder, I met with a group of friends in my community to discuss what we could do to make the world a better place. We decided to start a daily email newsletter to offer readers stories of kindness. We called the newsletter "A Daily Dose of Kindness" and our organization "Partners in Kindness."

We created an email list of 150 of our friends and relatives. People on the list sent me descriptions of acts of kindness that they had observed. I edited and distributed them. Subscribers received a daily email featuring a different kindness story each day.

After a few months, we introduced a second email called "Kind Words," which was syndicated, free of charge, around the world. In addition to stories, these emails also contained scientific insights on kindness and sensitivity enhancement techniques.

When we established the emails, one of the rules we had was that the author's identity would not be revealed. Altruists usually prefer this, since they try to avoid bragging and they prefer that others do not know about their kind deeds. Therefore, most of the stories contained in this book have been entered anonymously.

Another rule was that we would not reveal the identity of the recipient of an act of kindness, since the person or persons might be embarrassed because of poverty, illness, or some other misfortune. Therefore, in a few of the stories contained in this book, facts such as names, genders, ages and locations, as well as any other details that could identify the kindness recipient were either changed or omitted.

(When I once made the mistake of not changing the number of children in a large family, I received several angry emails from subscribers who explained that the details in the story clearly identified the family. They told me that the family would be horrified and terribly embarrassed if they saw this story about them.)

A World of Kindness, One Person at a Time

Although the stories appear anonymously, I forward any comments that I receive to the authors. Reading these comments excites them to do even greater acts of kindness and to spread our kindness message. A woman in Baltimore was so excited by the comments that she decided to start a column in her local newspaper. Another woman described how seeing her story published in one of our emails inspired and empowered her:

It is very tickling and strange to see my own words coming back to me from your "Daily Dose [of Kindness]." I hope others, when they read these, can see how important it is to implement the small changes in ourselves and that we, on our own, can really make a difference in the world. We each can spread kindness, initiating the ripple effect, spreading it all over the world!

The emails are a powerful force to spread kindness and propagate a chain reaction. When subscribers are inspired by a story, they often send that story to everyone on their own email contact list. A woman in the Philippines forwards the emails to every email list in her country. Another woman makes 70 photocopies of our daily email for all the congregants of her church who don't have email. A teacher in Hatfield, Massachusetts shares them with her writing groups. A teacher in Texas includes our emails in the program she teaches in women's prisons. Participants in her program, in turn, pass the material to other women who are not enrolled.

The emails are spreading far and wide. Over the past five years, Partners in Kindness has granted permission for our stories and kindness techniques to appear in eight languages in print and electronic media reaching a circulation of more than 1.5 million readers on six continents.

Inspiring Others with My Story

As a victim of terrorism, people want to hear my story. I am in a unique position to convey a message of hope and to improve the lives of others. Speaking in public and even emailing a description of my response to tragedy is an effective way to encourage others to subscribe to my emails. The emails, in turn, provide our readers with more stories as well as tools to cope with and overcome life's challenges.

People are fascinated by my ability to cope with tragedy. They are even more impressed by my positive response to terrorism. Whenever I speak to groups, during my highly interactive presentation, I ask the audience what their responses would be if a loved one was killed in an act of terrorism. The most common responses are "hatred" and "anger." Teaching kindness is indeed a very unusual response.

I discuss the way that I have transformed the horrible feelings brought about by terrorism into something beautiful by creating programs to teach kindness.

I may well be the only terror victim who does not focus on anger and hatred. I give a completely positive talk through a series of stories. I love telling stories and emphasizing the emotional aspects to the crowd and my audiences love it as well. Most of the participants come away feeling excited about doing something good.

It is only human to compare your life to the lives of others. When I speak, many of the participants put themselves in my position and wonder how I can be so positive. It is usually discussed in the question period after the lecture. My positive outlook in the face of tragedy and the discussions afterward are the most important part of my appearances.

Everyone has tragedies in their lives at one time or another—the breakup of relationships, the loss of loved ones, illness, poverty, and loneliness. The goal of my talk is to teach the audience how to transform the negativity of tragedies into something tremendously positive.

I talk about the effects our kindness emails have on people

living in the Middle East. Thousands of our subscribers in Israel are using the emails not only to cope with the fear of terror, but to become more sensitive and caring. When the situation was very bad in Israel, I frequently received emails from people who explained that before they had received the emails they had lost hope and felt paralyzed. The emails had restored their faith in humanity and inspired them to help others.

A few months after we started sending out our kindness emails—less than a year after September 11—a large Moslem charity in Kuwait contacted us and asked permission to forward our stories throughout their country. The emails are helping people to make a better world.

The Daily Dose of Kindness emails help people to put their lives in perspective and thereby both cope with difficult circumstances and grow in their ability to help others. They show readers that there are people all over the world who have less than they do and who know less than they do but who give of themselves more.

In my travels, I can see that the emails are encouraging leaders around the world to make greater contributions to their communities by instilling in them a new positive attitude. The "leaders" that I am referring to are not the politicians. They are the volunteers who are the first ones to raise their hands to help in communal organizations and other non-profit groups. They are the people you don't read about in newspapers, because they purposely don't want anyone to know about the kind deeds that they do. They are the idealists first and foremost who want to make the world a better place.

When I have the opportunity to speak, my excitement for kindness is infectious, as this student from New York City's Stuyvesant High School explains:

I walked into Lecture Hall A today, expecting to attend the lecture given by Shmuel Greenbaum for one period. I ended up staying for four. It is so uplifting, so enlightening, so refreshing to hear someone like him talk, to simply bubble over with excitement at the thought of doing good in the world. He is in his way a role model to us all. You think to yourself, "If only everyone else could practice kindness in the way that Shmuel Greenbaum has, the world would truly be a better place."

When people who have experienced challenging life experiences see someone who has overcome one of life's bitterest challenges, it allows them to view their situation in a better perspective. It gives them moral strength, a sense of purpose, and a feeling of being able to control their destinies.

And Now, the Good News

When the news on TV, on the radio, and in the newspapers is filled with violence, it's not only the victims of violence who think the world is a cruel place—we all become exposed to that way of thinking—we all become victims of violence. We feel helpless and depressed. We lose faith in humanity and feel there is nothing that we can do to make the world better.

On the other hand, when we are exposed to people doing good things, it reminds us of the good things that we have done in the past and the good things that others have done for us. By bombarding a person with positive emails, we can counteract those negative feelings. Positive emails make a person think, "The world is filled with good people and I want to be one, too."

It's hard to escape bad news in the media. Some readers tell us that our emails help them to forget about the bad and just focus on the good. Anne from California explains:

It just struck me today as I was reading the Daily Dose of Kindness that I love so much, that I had just read several news reports of what is going on in the world and they had had a rather depressing effect on me. Then I read your "kindness" column, and it just lifted me up, once again, to be reading about the good things people are doing for each other in a world that seems to concentrate on the bad. Thank you for helping to make my day, and I'm sure the day of many, many others."

The emails empower readers to not only tackle their own problems, but to reach out and make the world better, as Julia Bail of Washington, D.C. comments:

Reading the Kindness letters... gives me more hope for mankind than anything else in my life.

Role Models for the Next Generation

The importance of modeling positive behavior to children cannot be underestimated. The stories of overcoming difficulties and focusing on others are very often used to inspire young people, explains Jill Goldstein, a Florida college student studying in New York City:

I don't recall how I started receiving the "Kind Words" emails, but I love them. They are filled with stories that speak from the hearts of the kind of people with whom I wish to surround myself. More importantly, it's great that these stories are told by observers... people who SEE these acts of kindness and recognize them, even if they are not directly involved.

This summer I was in charge of programming for 9th grade campers at Camp Coleman in Cleveland, Georgia, with the theme "Repairing the World" and I often used these stories as examples. Perhaps more than anything else, these stories have changed me and the kindness has trickled down through me to other staff and the campers.

Two years ago, a Unit Head for the 9th graders who came from Sderot, Israel had a tragedy hit very close to him. One day, we returned very late and he was called to the office, where he was told that a rocket had hit the home of his best friend and that she was the only fatality in the attack. He was upset for days, but did not return to Israel.

The support from the entire camp was amazing but he said the one thing that brought him out of the slump was the simple smiles of his campers. Kids who had not even been to high school yet, many who are from very well-off families, came together for their head counselor. They surprised him by planning to plant a tree of life in memory of the girl and in honor of their Unit Head. They made a plaque and held a dedication ceremony.

A housewife named Sarah Chana explains how the stories give her strength to care for her children and energy to stay up at all hours:

It takes a lot of strength, patience, and enthusiasm to raise children. Thank you for this lovely email. This one has me in tears (it's only 4:15 a.m.!!) and I'm highly motivated. It's time to go to the kitchen, and bake something for some kids who are having a hard time. What a victory it will be! (Even though the kids are mine...!)

Improving Society

The kindness project I started in the aftermath of my wife's murder is improving society. Subscribers are writing about their experiences and reading about the efforts of others who serve as role models for them. The stories are showing them that there really are good people in the world and inspiring them to be one of them.

Since our emails often show how people have overcome different types of crises, they have provided our readers with a catalyst for personal growth. The stories show us the power of kindness to transform us into better, more compassionate human beings.

Gratitude

When faced with tragedy we can respond in one of two ways; we can either react with bitterness for what we have lost or with gratitude for what we still have. I have chosen the path of gratitude. I thank God for giving me the strength to make this choice and for providing so many people to help me teach kindness to others. But most of all I thank God for giving me my wife, Shoshana, a true role model of kindness and the inspiration for this book.

I am grateful to all of the people who helped with this book; to the hundreds of volunteers who contributed stories, edited text and provided financial and emotional support; to my parents and my in-laws who have always been there for me with love and advice; to my spiritual advisors, whose modesty prevents me from mentioning their names.

In Love with Israel

This book illustrates the inner beauty of Israel. It reveals the love that the people of Israel have for each other and the loving acts of kindness that they do as a result of this love. The stories are about, and from, people of all religions throughout the world as well as in Israel. The entries were written by one hundred contributors out of a total 33,000 email subscribers. There are several reasons why we chose to focus on Israel in the book:

◇ When I looked at all the stories that have been submitted to Partners in Kindness over the years, I found that Israel was the most common topic.

◇ My wife, Shoshana had a tremendous love for Israel and she was killed, as well as buried, in Israel.

◇ The first chapter of my life ended in Israel. Now it is only appropriate that the second chapter begin with Israel.

◇ The Land of Israel and the People of Israel have a special place in the hearts of people of many different religions.

◇ Public opinion polls indicate that people are interested in learning more about Israel and the Middle East. This is also confirmed by the news media's constant focus on that area of the world.

◇ Almost all of the news stories about Israel and the Middle East are negative. This book presents positive stories.

◇ Showing the world the positive stories may bring new hope to Israel and the Middle East.

Spirituality

Since Israel is the spiritual center for the world's three major monotheistic religions and many of the stories have been written by spiritual people, a few of the stories in this book contain spiritual content.

One of our biggest fans who even helped to edit this book, Linda Hernandez, is a Christian Pastoral Counselor in Peoria, Illinois. Linda explains that people of all religions will enjoy the stories from this book:

> *The stories are helpful and encouraging to everyone, especially those experiencing difficult times. I know that in pastoral care, which I do, such a resource is often helpful. I cannot help but think that this book could be of help to many, not only Jewish people. After all, I have received much from the entries. It is a real testimony to the saying that "actions speak louder than words." God may have bigger ideas for this book than you ever imagined.*

Interestingly enough, quite a few of our atheist subscribers have told me how much they love our stories because they make them feel spiritually uplifted.

The Language and Style

Since very few stories in this book were written by professional writers, the stories have been edited and simplified, so that even young children can enjoy reading them. In the editing process, every attempt has been made to preserve the communication style of the author. Most foreign words and phrases are followed by a translation. A glossary is provided for those foreign words and phrases which are not followed by a translation.

Style of the Stories

The style of the stories is often different from popular story books with which you may be familiar. This offers several advantages:

Most of the stories are short and to the point without lengthy lead-ins. Stories written in other books sometimes require a great deal of stressful concentration and analysis.

Since the stories in our book are short, simple, and to the point, they are relaxing to read, especially after a stressful day or before the start of a stressful day. The readers of our emails have told us that they much prefer this type of style because they are very busy people and they have very little free time.

This style allows busy people to get a quick "moral boost" and then move on to their next task.

This style is especially helpful for younger readers who have limited attention spans and reading skills.

Each story demonstrates a concrete act that the reader can do to make the world better. One popular book suggests in its introduction that the lessons to be learned from its stories are not always clear. The authors go on to recommend that the reader hire them to conduct a workshop in which they will explain the lessons.

Since the purpose of this book is to make the world better, the acts needed to do so are stated simply and clearly. No costly follow-ups are necessary.

While every effort was made to pick the most interesting stories, some of the stories may not interest you. Since everyone has different needs and interests, different stories will resonate with different people. In sending out our "Daily Dose of Kindness" emails, I have found that it is often the stories that I like the least which generate the most positive feedback.

Every story has been carefully selected to be family friendly. There is no need to worry about stories that are not appropriate for children. Every story imparts positive moral values.

How to Use this Book

As the title implies, each story is "A Daily Dose of Kindness." While there is no danger of overdosing by reading more than one story a day, the prescribed dosage to reach maximum effectiveness is one story per day. This dosage will help you remember the story, think about it all day and internalize the message, then relate it to others.

Taking your "Daily Dose of Kindness" at night before you go to sleep can help you to forget about the negative things that occurred during the day, and focus on the positive things. Used in this manner, it can help you to sleep better.

Your "Daily Dose of Kindness" can be the perfect thing to help you to relax for a minute or two before work or school.

Sharing your "Daily Dose of Kindness" with others during meal times can help to stimulate wonderful conversations with friends and family.

Since everyone loves a good story, relating a story from the book at social functions can help you "break the ice." It could give your social life a boost and may even help your career.

You can share your "Daily Dose of Kindness" with children before they go to sleep, when you want them to sit quietly, or when you just want to relax and enjoy their company. Each story will give them a quick moral lesson that they can think about, internalize and act upon.

Teachers can read a story to their students and use it as a springboard to discuss acts of kindness, intercultural issues, world politics, or spiritual topics.

Public speakers can include a story in one of their speeches to motivate their audiences and pick up their spirits. The stories can help anyone become a gifted public speaker.

What Else Can You Do?

Make a difference in your life. Subscribe to our emails at: www.PartnersInKindness.org and www.TraditionOfKindness.org.

Make a difference in your family. Read "A Daily Dose of Kindness" with your family. The stories can stimulate conversations and they can help your family to share their emotions and values.

Make a difference in the people you care about. Send them our emails and send them a copy of this book for a special occasion or for no occasion at all. Just tell them how much you care about them and how you hope they will enjoy this book.

Make a difference to people in Israel. Contact kindness organizations in Israel listed at the end of this book (page 272).

Watch our emails for information on the release of our second book - *Lessons from Terrorism: The Science of Kindness.* This book will look at the latest breakthroughs in scientific research on kindness. Scientists will explain how these emails are improving people's lives and have the potential to impact many more people around the world.

Make a difference to a group of people. Invite me to speak. Contact info@PartnersInKindness.org.

Make a difference in the world. Ask the news media to focus on the good and join us as Partners in Kindness.

The Business
of Kindness

∽╶╳╫╫╟╌∾

The Power of Kindness
By Bracha Jaffe

My husband David called me on my cell phone the week before our daughter's wedding and told me, "We have a wrinkle."

The electric company had posted a notice on our apartment building announcing a power outage in our neighborhood to allow for a major repair. The problem was that it fell out exactly on the day of the wedding.

I called the electric company to ask, or rather beg, them to postpone the repair work, since we really, really needed our apartment to prepare for the wedding (makeup, hair, etc.). I was immediately transferred to a manager named Zion. He understood the problem and explained that they absolutely couldn't reschedule the power outage, but he would see what he could do.

Two days later, he said that he had sent some people out to look at the site but they were having trouble isolating our building from the rest of the area. But, not to worry, if he couldn't resolve the problem, we could have a room in the electric company's building to use as we wished! I was flabbergasted and asked if he'd ever seen a bride leave from the electric company. He said, "Actually, it's happened before."

The next day he called, and in a happy voice conveyed his best wishes for the upcoming wedding. He asked me to tell the bride "*mazal tov*," and promised she would have electricity because he personally went to look at the location and found a solution.

So we got up bright and early on Sunday morning, and lo

and behold, there was a generator parked right outside of our building. That's right—27 Schvartz Street was hooked up to electricity all day from our own private generator while the rest of the neighborhood had a blackout! It was amazing. There are truly people here with big hearts. They made it clear that our happiness was important to them as well.

We sent a warm "thank you" letter to the electric company along with some wonderful pictures. I sent this story to some newspapers and it actually appeared in the *Yediot* supplement with a picture of the generator outside our building. Kindness is still alive and well in Israel.

When People Care More about People Than about Money, it Makes All the Difference

One of the places you might least expect to see acts of kindness is in the business world. I am grateful for the kindness of people with whom I have had the privilege of working, while launching a new business.

One person offered to loan me, interest-free, the money I needed to produce a new product, in case the production costs would not be covered by advance orders.

Another person made sure his work assignment was completed on time, even though he was told it could wait because he had been hospitalized for a medical procedure.

Someone else volunteered to do extra work so the project would be perfect, although he had already received payment for completing his assignment.

Another person donated his offices for our staff meetings, because the location was more convenient.

Then there's my neighbor who fixed my computer at no charge, and my colleagues who phoned and emailed me a few extra times to express their caring when they knew I was having a hard day.

Running a business is hard sometimes, but when people care more about people than they do about money, it makes all the difference....

What is Your Dream?

I wanted to write this story because I am amazed at how much power believing in someone generates. When someone believed in me, it changed my life.

For many years I have been leading groups for parents and parents-to-be. Six years ago, I decided to publish some books and materials that parents find very helpful, beginning with a book called, *How to Talk So Kids Will Listen and Listen So Kids Will Talk* by Faber and Mazlish. Since the original material was written in English, I decided to purchase the Hebrew language rights to the book. A woman named Maya, whom I barely knew, offered to give me a loan to get started. Her sole interest was her belief in the project. We have since become close friends.

After publishing the first book in Hebrew, I walked, hitch-hiked, and took buses and taxis to everyone I could think of who would be interested in the topic of raising children. I lugged suitcases of materials to Eilat, Kiryat Shmona, Hashmonaim, Jerusalem, Bat Yam and any other place where groups of people were willing to listen.

When I thought I had exhausted my list of contacts, I met yet another person who asked, "How are you going to fulfill your mission?" He gave me the phone number of a friend who he said could help. I made yet another phone call and an appointment with Eitan, who also came to believe in my project.

"What is your dream?" he asked. I had no clear answer because my dream was still too ambiguous.

Over the next six years, I came to define a clear vision of my dream. I also came to realize that believing in myself was a slow process that took time to evolve. I developed a deep appreciation for the people who came into my life, who believed in me, and reminded me over and over again, "Never give up" and "Believe in yourself—I believe in you." During these years we have published five more books, reprinted them many times, trained new group leaders, and continued to organize many more groups.

Dreaming is essential for bringing goodness into reality. Dreaming becomes practical when you know how to define your dream, how to plan and delegate, and what steps to take to in order to turn the dream into reality. Fulfilling dreams is possible when people believe in you.

When someone believes in you, you feel it. It gives you the energy, drive and conviction to keep on going even when things aren't going the way you hoped they would. Believing in someone is powerful.

Compassion Instead of Anger

After a colleague of mine signed a contract with me, he spoke to me in an insulting and harsh way because of something he misunderstood in the contract.

I decided to listen quietly without reacting, and said, "I need some time to think this over." I was so angered and hurt, that my first thought was to cancel the contract and stop working with him.

I waited several days until my anger dissipated. Then I heard from a mutual friend that this person's daughter had suddenly taken ill and was hospitalized.

I called to wish her a speedy recovery, wrote down the child's name to pray for her, and gave charity. Needless to say, he was very grateful for the phone call and for the support.

Finding a way to be kind and giving helped me to feel compassion instead of anger towards this man.

After his daughter has a full recovery, with God's help, I am sure we will be able to resolve our difference over the contract in a peaceful way so that we can continue working together.

⌒ⵊⵊⵊⵊⵊ⌒

A Wonderful Lesson in Life

I had so many things to do the other day; I didn't know how I would get them all done. My first stop was the bank. When I arrived, there was a death notice on the door. The father of one of the tellers had passed away.

I knew the deceased was the father of the teller who takes care of my account because the last time I was at the bank, she told me that her father had been diagnosed suddenly with terminal cancer. As I sat and listened to her, she cried and told me about her family. I never finished taking care of my errands that day.

As I recalled that conversation, I asked for the address of the *beit shivah* (house of mourning), jotted it down, and went on to my business meeting.

When the meeting was over, I changed my plans for the rest of the day and drove to the *beit shivah* to visit my teller and her family. She showed me pictures of her father, many of them with his grandchildren around him. There were several pictures of the last days of his life. His family had surrounded him with love and attention. As she talked about her family, I could feel the great respect and adoration she felt for her father and for her mother who had passed away years earlier. You could see in the pictures how this great respect and caring for parents and grandparents had passed from generation to generation.

As I was getting ready to leave, she asked me several questions about Jewish laws and customs regarding mourning. After some discussion, I put her in touch with a rabbi who could help. From outward appearances, you could say that she was "secular" and I was "religious." On a deeper level, we were simply two women, each of us doing our best, both with the desire to give to others. While I performed the kindness of visiting and comforting a mourner, I received a great lesson in respecting one's parents and grandparents.

I don't now remember what my original plans were for that day. But I do know that if I hadn't changed them, I would have always looked back and felt sorry that I had missed a chance to do a kindness for someone and at the same time receive a wonderful lesson in life.

〜〜〜

The Music of Kindness

My daughter wanted to take music lessons at the community center in Gush Etzion. She asked us if she could study the drums, but we did not want to have drums in our house. So we convinced her to study the *chalil*, a recorder-like front-facing flute. I spoke to the teacher in advance so that he would know she has low self-esteem and loses her temper quickly.

During the short tryout/interview, her teacher was absolutely amazing. He was very complimentary of her and built up her self-esteem. She was so happy with him that she forgot about her dream of playing the drums and was looking forward to *chalil* lessons with this wonderful man. He told her that she would do well with the *chalil*, but he thought the drums would be the perfect instrument for her and recommended the drum teacher at the community center.

Her face lit up, but I was in shock. I had not told him she wanted to play drums. How did he know? When I asked him, he explained that her command of beat and rhythm led him to think she would be great at drums. He later explained to me that it is an excellent way to direct all her "excess" energy and he thought it would be very beneficial for her in general. When I explained to him that we did not want drums in our house, he told me that the center has a drum room that kids enrolled in classes can reserve for practice.

Though my daughter wanted very much to play drums, she got so attached to this wonderful teacher in ten minutes that she was not convinced she should study drums after all. When we explained this to him, his reply was that he is always here, always available to talk to, and if she ever decides she has had enough of drums she could go to him for lessons.

He did so much for her in such a short time. We were amazed at his wisdom in suggesting she study drums, which was her dream. But what most impressed us was that he gave up a paying student in order to do what was best for her.

There Aren't Many People Like You

Recently, I forgot my car keys in a curtain store in Talpiot, Jerusalem. When I went back to the store there was a sign saying the owner had left early to go to a wedding.

Since I am from Haifa, I panicked. I couldn't ask anyone to go to my house and send me my spare set of keys by taxi because we had just changed the lock and no one had a spare key!

Fortunately, I caught the owner on his cell phone. He came back in his wedding attire and opened the store for me. And I got my keys back.

I was so grateful that the next time I came to Jerusalem I bought him a bottle of wine. He was so touched. He said "There aren't many people like you."

I told him "I beg to differ. There aren't many people like you!"

A Moving Experience

I needed to transport a set of sofas within Jerusalem and was looking for a mini-mover service. I remembered someone I had used some twenty-three years ago who had come highly recommended and was really nice. I looked up the name in the White Pages and called. The man was still there, but told me he was no longer in that business and that, offhand, he couldn't think of anyone to recommend.

Shortly after I hung up, the man called me back. He had searched the Yellow Pages, found someone he knew and trusted, and called to give me the name and telephone number.

When I hung up, I was suffused with a feeling of warmth. It's great to share this world with people who love to perform acts of kindness.

⚌⚌⚌

A Large Fly and a Kind-Hearted Guy

My son witnessed the following:

While some teenage girls were standing and chatting at the local shopping center, a large fly landed on one of the girls, sending her into a mild panic. She slipped and fell, banging her head on the stairs. She was clearly not really injured, but startled nonetheless.

Immediately a young man behind the counter at a nearby ice cream shop came over with an ice pop for her head and a bottle of cold water.

⚌⚌⚌

Soldiers on the House

I studied for a few weeks in the Old City in Jerusalem. One day, during a break, I was sitting in the Menorah Café, writing post-cards. Before I had time to order, I had to leave to go back to my classes. I promised the owner I would come back for a meal. He said it was not necessary.

Although I almost forgot, I made sure to come back, since I felt obliged to buy something. I was rewarded by getting to see an incredible act of kindness. About ten soldiers came into the café and ordered. The owner did not take any money from them, despite the difficult times (the intifada had greatly reduced the number of tourists)!

After seeing that, I thanked the owner for teaching me a lesson in kindness with his actions. I made it a point to return often to the café to order whatever I could in order to give this wonderful gentleman the business he so justly deserved.

I have told this story a number of times and everyone I told it was to appreciate this man's incredible kindness.

ᗧᨏᨏᨏᗨ

Money in the Bank

One of the tellers in my local bank was assisting me when she received a call on her cell phone from her husband. She politely asked me to excuse her for a brief moment, and took the call. When she was finished, she told me that her husband had given her the names of two children in their daughter's class whose parents were unable to pay the fee for the school's year-end outing, and had asked her to transfer money from their personal account into the school's account to cover the fee for the two children.

The teller completed my transaction, apologizing for the interruption, and then made the transfer that her husband had requested. She then called the school's secretary and notified her that the money had been placed in the school's account.

One can only imagine how these children might have felt if they had been unable to participate in the class trip, especially for lack of funds. One can also imagine the joy they must have felt upon learning that the expense had been anonymously covered.

An Uplifting Experience

I went to my local supermarket in Ashkelon during the week of Passover. When I returned to my car with a cart full of food, I realized my key was missing. I asked in the store and also retraced my steps, but still no key. I told the two security guards outside the store that I didn't know what to do. One of them asked me to show him which car was mine. He peeped through the window and saw my keys on the passenger seat. I had made the mistake of locking the doors without making sure I had the key. One problem solved, but now what do I do?

The guard saw an electrician working next door and asked him if he had a wire they could ease through a tiny space in the back window and maybe manage to lift up the lock button.

The electrician left everything and started trying to rescue my key. After ten minutes, I wanted to release him, since he was getting phone calls about other work on his cell phone and was telling everyone he was busy at the moment. But he was determined and kept saying, "With God's help, we are going to get that key out." A mentally retarded young adult came to help, and patiently provided shade so the electrician could see what he was doing.

Forty-five minutes later, after trying all sorts of ingenious ideas, he fished out the key by using a long metal wire as a fishing rod. Then he opened the door with the key and wished me a happy holiday and went back to his work.

I then locked the doors (WITH THE KEY!) and ran back into the shop to buy chocolates for them. Neither the guard nor my "savior" (appropriately named Michael, the name of an angel) wanted to accept them and said they had done nothing. The young shade provider had disappeared as suddenly as he had appeared.

Throughout the entire time, all the passers-by sympathized and each and every one of them told me it had happened to them at some point and they recalled how annoying it was. But thanks to the kindness of Ilan the guard, Michael "the angel" and Lior "the shade," it wasn't annoying but an "uplifting" experience for me—and also for the key.

Feeding the Hungry

Diverse Cultures United by a Love for Israel

My brother and sister-in-law began volunteering in the Beit Levenstein Hospital in Ra'anana, Israel. They visit victims of terror attacks and other horrible events.

One of the young men they were visiting was a Bedouin IDF (Israel Defense Forces) soldier who had been very seriously wounded. He complained that one of the things he missed most was familiar food. For someone used to eating Bedouin food (foods of Arab origin), it was really a hardship.

My sister-in-law phoned an Israeli Arab friend who works in a nearby supermarket, and explained the situation to him. She told him to bring some fresh food from his village the next day and she would pay for it.

The next day he turned up at the door with four full bags of delicacies. When she asked how much she owed him, he said, "Oh, no. This is for one of our soldiers. It's the least we could do."

Teenage Boy in the Kitchen

When I read about all these charities, I never know how much to believe. One of your stories mentioned Hazon Yeshaya—a soup kitchen, for lack of a better description.

My fifteen-year-old son enjoys volunteering and asked me

to find things for him to do this summer. As I called, I kept hearing the name Hazon Yeshaya. So I got the contact information for him.

He's been there all week. In fact, he's been waking up earlier than usual. One morning, I asked him why he was up so early. He replied, "There is a lot of work to do!"

He peels vegetables, checks rice, packs food, and more. He comes home pretty tired, and not too clean, but he is really enjoying himself.

When I told one of my email friends in the U.S. about what he was doing, she recommended it to her son here in Israel.

Table to Table

My friend's husband started an organization in Ra'anana, Israel, called Table to Table. Many volunteers, including my husband, go out late at night to collect untouched leftover food from catering halls and establishments and deliver it to the Table to Table warehouse for distribution, or deliver it to the soup kitchens directly. Along the lines of America's City Harvest, Table to Table hopes to grow beyond the boundaries of Israel's Sharon Region, providing meals throughout Israel to those who most need them.

⸎

When an Opportunity to Help Presents Itself, Grab It!

Many years ago, on one of my first trips to Israel from America, I was enthralled with the atmosphere in Geula, Jerusalem. New to me were the beggars on the side of the street, waiting and hoping for passers-by to drop coins into their outstretched hands.

Although this happened thirty years ago, I still remember one beggar, an elderly woman, who approached me, asking for a few coins so she could collect enough money to buy a drink. We were standing near the entrance of a crowded kiosk. I invited her to come inside with me, and ordered a glass of freshly squeezed orange juice for her.

I still remember the look of gratitude on her face, and felt a similar joy and gratitude in being able to do something nice for this elderly woman. I learned an important lesson from this experience—when an opportunity presents itself to help another person and give them a little (or a lot!) of happiness or pleasure, grab it! It's a special moment that you'll treasure your whole life.

Extremists in Gratitude and Kindness

Many soldiers are stationed near our home in Gush Etzion (a community located twenty minutes south of Jerusalem). It is customary that whenever people have extra food they stop by the soldiers' stations on their way to Jerusalem, to deliver plates of cake or food to the hungry soldiers. The soldiers are always thrilled with anything they receive.

In memory of two men that were killed by terrorists (Tzachi Sasson and Dr. Shmuel Gillis), their widows opened a "cozy corner" in a mobile home at the main junction. Here all the soldiers in the area, as well as all those passing through, can go to get hot and cold drinks, soups, snacks and home-baked cake. All the residents bake and deliver the freshly baked items to this cozy corner, and it is "manned" or "womanned" about eighteen hours a day. Residents come from as far as Beit Shemesh to bring cakes. We often get two hundred soldiers a day. It's not only the food that they enjoy—they love the care and attention they receive from our volunteers.

As time goes on, more and more is donated to this cozy corner. For the soldiers' break time, we now have a TV and VCR, and an industrial size popcorn maker. An array of card games, chess, backgammon, and other games are also available.

The residents are glad to show thanks to the soldiers protecting us and the soldiers are thrilled to see that they are appreciated. The media often portrays the residents living over the Green Line (which marks Israel's pre-1967 border) as being extremists, so it is especially important to us for these soldiers to see what type of people we really are—extremists in gratitude and kindness.

❦

Treats for All the Soldiers

I discovered that my married son was doing army reserve duty with a unit of sixty soldiers, only half an hour away from our home.

I baked a huge batch of cookies, packed a bag of fruit and chocolates, and drove out to bring it to my son. We agreed to meet on his patrol route by the gate of one of the communities the unit is guarding. We were able to speak for a few minutes, and he smiled in appreciation of the treats for all the soldiers.

As I drove away, I was filled with a sense of awe of the blessings bestowed on us—the land which we have been given to cultivate and protect, and our magnificent children who appreciate what they have been given and who are ready to serve their people with all their heart and soul. As I looked in my rear view mirror, I noticed that my son's patrol jeep was following me out to the main road, making sure I arrived safely.

⌐╌╌╌╌

Enough Food to Feed an Army

At the close of the holiday of Rosh Hashanah, Ari Weiss, of blessed memory, called home from Shechem (Nablus) to tell his mother that he and his unit of thirty-five soldiers had been on a difficult mission over the holiday. All they had to eat was what they had been able to carry in their pockets—*challah,* humus, and some candy.

Susan immediately went out to the main street and walked to the *shwarma* (meat) restaurant where her son frequently ate with his friends. She told the restaurant manager the story. He asked her: "How many?" "Thirty-five," she replied. He quickly prepared thirty-five portions of *shwarma* and packed it up for the unit.

Feeling very encouraged, Susan went to the next store and told the manager the story. He asked her the same question: "How many?" "Thirty-five," she replied. He quickly packed a case of beverages for the hungry soldiers.

Susan continued on her way down the main street to the bakery. The baker asked the same question: "How many?" "Thirty-five," she said once more. Within a short time, she had packages of cookies and honey cakes for each soldier, along with the sandwiches and drinks.

Arranging transport to Ariel in the Shomron was easy, and the army sent a jeep from Shechem to Ariel to pick up the food and bring it back to the soldiers. Of course, the jeep driver was shocked at the quantity of food cases he had to load into his jeep. Apparently he was expecting to pick up a few sandwiches, and instead found that he had to transport enough food to feed an army!

A short while later Susan received a phone call from Ari. He called to thank her on behalf of the whole unit. In the background she could hear them laughing and shouting "thank-you!" Mission Accomplished.

Last week Rabbi Stuart and Susan Weiss received the heartbreaking news that their son, Ari, was killed in Shechem when he and his unit had uncovered a terrorist base. At his funeral, which was attended by thousands, one of the speakers said he now understood why Ari cared so much about everyone else and not just about himself. He came from a family who looked to give to others at every opportunity, and inspired others to do so, too. Some people wonder how it is possible to go on living after such a tragic loss. I believe the Weiss family and others like them will show us all the way to continue living through their constant giving to others.

Children of
Israel

Curing with Love

At the beginning of the school year, one of my sixteen-year-old daughter's classmates discovered he had leukemia and started treatment. All the students in his grade wanted to do something beyond giving him personal encouragement and visiting him.

They asked the staff at the hospital where he was being treated (which was far away from where we all live) how they could help. They were told that the hospital needed an early detection machine which costs a few hundred thousand shekels.

These kids rolled up their sleeves and got to work. They got various jobs and donated their income—they cleaned cars, sold donated flowers, and organized a pop concert by a famous Israeli singer that raised tens of thousands of shekels from ticket sales and donations in one magnificent evening. They also organized a soccer game with well-known players.

They came up with such original ideas. One girl charged other girls for foot massages; others crocheted *kippot (yarmulkas)* and scarves and sold them.

In addition to hearing about these impressive acts of kindness to raise money towards a lifesaving machine, this pupil has seen boundless love and commitment displayed by his classmates. It has no doubt planted a joy and optimism in his heart that will help him recover. We are indeed blessed to see our children showing such loving initiative.

During the modest ceremony at the school a year later, when the pupils handed over the check, the head of the department of pediatric oncology was overcome with emotion. He explained that he had attended many check-receiving ceremonies but had never been moved to tears the way he was when he saw these wonderful young people and all they had accomplished over the course of a year's unrelenting activity.

He told them how much easier it would be for the hospital to raise the rest of the costs, when they could tell donors that eleventh-graders in one school had raised over half the cost of the life-saving machinery. Moreover, he had no doubt that their acts of love and support were an immeasurable and over-whelming force in their classmate's recuperation.

⌐₩∭⌐

Kindness in the Headlines

As I was leaving our local grocery store today, my eye caught the headline of the daily newspaper, on sale near the entrance of the store. It was too shocking to repeat.

When I arrived home, my seventeen-year-old son had just returned from five days of volunteer work in Kfar Yavetz with sixteen of his friends. Imagine a newspaper headline, "Seventeen teenage boys on their summer vacation volunteer to help a struggling community."

His hands still stained with yellow paint from painting fences, he told us how they had prepared fields for planting, in-stalled sprinkler systems for agriculture, and planted fields of cabbage.

They worked long hours in the hot sun with the joy of a

sense of purpose and commitment. The next time they get together in their meeting room, they'll be discussing their next project. No doubt, it will make an inspiring newspaper headline.

Thank you for allowing us to read this uplifting news in your *Daily Dose of Kindness* emails!

Kindness in the Closet

One evening, I entered my bedroom and found that the rod that held all of the clothing in my closet had fallen down, and all of the dresses, skirts, blouses and jackets were lying in a pile on the floor. The plastic hardware supporting the rod had cracked and broken, creating quite a messy scene. I laughed and hoped this was a *kapparah*—spiritual cleansing for something.

The following day, I bought the necessary hardware for repairing and re-hanging the rod. When I came home, my daughter was waiting, tools in hand, to install it. She had already neatly sorted the clothing into two piles. "Mom, I organized your clothing so that one can be put back into the closet, and the other, which hasn't been worn in a long time, can be donated to charity, so that it can be enjoyed by others!"

It is true that I pushed less worn clothing to the back of the closet, thinking it would have use in the future. I appreciated her thoughtfulness—and her tact.

Kindergarten Birthday Kindness

We have an organization that gives workshops to groups of parents and teachers throughout Israel. A mother in one of our groups told us that in the kindergarten which her child attends, whenever one of the children has a birthday, he or she is responsible for thinking of a kindness project that all the children of the kindergarten can do together.

We thought this was such a beautiful idea, that we asked this mother to bring a list of all the kindness projects that have been done by this kindergarten, so we could share it in our groups and encourage other parents and teachers to initiate such projects.

Since the Tradition of Kindness website was launched, we have became more aware and sensitized to the fact that kindness doesn't just come naturally, but must be continuously encouraged.

The following are kindness projects that are done on an ongoing basis by the five-year-old children of a kindergarten in the community of Eli in the Shomron. Each act of kindness is planned in honor of the birthday of one of the children, and the children themselves think of the project they would like to initiate for their birthdays.

◇ The children cleaned the gardens that belong to elderly people in the community, and planted flowers for them.

◇ On the holiday of TuB'Shvat, the New Year for trees, they prepared and distributed baskets of fruit to soldiers.

◇ The children, together with the elderly, decorated the community hall before Israel Independence Day.

◇ Prepared and decorated charity boxes for each child to take home.

◇ Made get-well cards and sent them to the children's ward in a hospital.

◇ Decorated washing cups to be distributed to different institutions.

◇ Prepared food parcels which were sent to needy families.

◇ The children made magnets on which was written, "With love, from the children of Gan Shaked in Eli" and attached them to packets of candies, which they sent to the children in Gush Katif. (This story took place while the government of Israel was planning to evacuate Gush Katif and the other Jewish communities in Gaza. For a further explanation see the chapter entitled, "The Cost of Peace: Tragedy in Gaza," page 231.)

◇ The children prepared a special gift for a mother who had given birth.

◇ The children invited soldiers to the kindergarten for a special program, and gave the soldiers candies.

Empathy Dispels Fear

My granddaughter went to kindergarten this week, very unwillingly. At first she cried and refused to participate. Her mother pointed to a girl who was younger and was also frightened to be there. My granddaughter then "adopted" this little girl, and tried to make her feel comfortable in the kindergarten. She now waits for her to come in the morning, saves a place for her on the bench, and makes sure she knows what's happening. It's very special to see a three-year-old show sensitivity and caring for others.

They Have Nothing and I Have Everything

These two stories are about my seven-year-old:

She took a painful blood test this week. The nurse had to prick her three times. In order to cheer my daughter up, before she left for school I gave her a big bar of white chocolate and suggested she not eat the entire bar herself. She came home after school and told me that she didn't eat any of it, because she gave it out to all of her friends!

Her closet was a mess, so we emptied everything out and went through it item by item, deciding what she wanted and what we would give away to poor people. Both piles grew, but as the pile for herself grew larger, she stopped and shook her head from side to side and said, "It isn't fair to the poor people. I'm taking too much. I have to give more to them. They have nothing and I have everything."

⌇⌇⌇

"Natan's Bike"

This message was posted on the Ramat Beit Shemesh email list:

Since the beginning of the riding season, our son Natan has desperately wanted a bicycle. We would have loved to give him a bike, but our circumstances did not permit it.

This morning Natan opened the front door to go to school, and there outside the door was a new bike with a sign which read "Natan's Bike."

We don't know who you are, but we hope you see this. You have given our son a great gift. He had a smile on his face, the likes of which we have not seen in a long time, and he literally floated out the door to the bus. We look forward to many happy afternoons of bike riding! Thank you for your generosity, your kindness and your sensitivity.

⌇⌇⌇

Leaving a Trail of Smiles
By Shulamit Wolfe Stander

Each of my children's *bar* and *bat mitzvah* celebrations was held at our home. For each one, we decorated the house in a motif using that child's favorite colors, with matching balloons. The day after each party, as we cleaned up and put the house back in order, the kids collected the balloons and formed large "bouquets," tied together with flowing ribbons.

The arrangements were beautiful, and we wanted to share them with others, so my kids and I took them to the pediatric ward at Sha'are Tzedek, our local Jerusalem hospital. During our first visit, I asked the head nurse to distribute them to the children who might benefit most from a "pick-me-up." However, she insisted that my children distribute the balloons to the patients themselves, rather than letting the staff do it, so the patients would feel that they had new friends.

The pride and joy that I felt watching my children distribute the bouquets was overwhelming. With each delivery, the patient's face would light up upon realizing that the beautiful arrangement was for him or her. My children left smiles where there were frowns, and sometimes stopped little ones from crying. I was particularly pleased that, at a time when so many children think mainly of themselves, my kids' were thinking of, and helping, others who were less fortunate!

A Special Party

Last night I attended a very special *bat mitzvah* here in Israel. The *bat mitzvah* girl had no father, and her family did not have the money to provide her with a party.

When the girl's teacher realized this, she offered to have a party for the class, in her home. One of the mothers felt it was not a good idea—after all, which child has a *bat mitzvah* party in her teacher's home? It would serve to emphasize to the child that she was different.

So the mother asked her local synagogue to provide their hall for free. Then she asked parents to donate what was necessary for a party.

When the owner of a catering firm was approached for a "special price," he immediately donated a full meal—chicken, schnitzel, salads, bread rolls, and cakes for dessert—all in such abundance that at the end of the evening there were lots of leftovers, which were immediately taken to a local charity for distribution to needy families.

Similarly a fancy *bat mitzvah* cake was donated, as well as drinks, and even small grace after meals booklets with the girl's name inscribed so that the guests could take home a reminder of the occasion as is customary.

Parents donated money for paper goods; the girl even had a new dress and was taken to the hair-dressing salon for this special occasion.

The school donated the services of a paid security guard (which we sadly need at even small public gatherings today). A teen band was taken to play live music (paid for by donations). Even a professional video camera man donated his services.

A few parents and older brothers and sisters came to decorate, lay out the food, serve, and join the festivities to make sure that it was a successful function. The tables were laid with everything—even decorative floral centerpieces.

There was nothing missing from this function. In fact, although everything was done modestly, it will be hard for the rest of the class to compete with such a successful function where all the children expressed such warmth for their less fortunate schoolmate and had such a good time!

A Celebration that Benefited Orphans

My niece just celebrated her *bat mitzvah*. My sister, who has been blessed with a successful career and is able to make sizable donations to charity, tries to instill the importance of charitable giving in her children. Toward this end, she suggested to my niece that guests invited to her *bat mitzvah* be asked to not give a traditional gift, but, instead, to donate to a charitable fund that would be established in honor of the event. Guests would have the option to choose a particular charity as the recipient of their gift, or to let the *bat mitzvah* girl decide where to donate the money. To my sister's delight, my niece endorsed the idea wholeheartedly. The fund was established, and they were thrilled to see that most of the guests followed the request on the invitation, rather than give a traditional gift. In fact, some of the guests who gave a gift also made a donation to the charitable fund.

My niece chose to donate all of the money in the fund to orphanages in Israel. My sister and I were particularly touched by her choice, because our grandmother, after whom my niece is named, spent her lifetime raising funds for Emuna and Mizrachi, organizations that operate homes for orphans, and my grandmother often said, "We must not forget the orphans in Israel." Interestingly, my niece was unaware of this bit of family history, yet made the same choice her grandmother would have made.

～♨♨♨～

Something to Raise Our Spirits

Yesterday was a sad day for us; one of the students in our *yeshiva* (seminary), Har Etzion in Alon Shevut, died from a terrorist attack. My husband returned from the funeral half an hour before the holiday of *Sukkos*. But something inspiring did happen today to help raise our spirits, and I wanted to share it.

Today a young girl celebrated her *bat mitzvah*. She follows in her talented mother's footsteps and designed a beautiful papercut artwork representing the return to Jerusalem, and with her own money, she had it reproduced. She chose a charity and advertised to the community that anyone who would make a donation to this charity would receive this beautiful piece of art. She specifically wanted to do something to help children, since she's a girl who knows what she wants. She chose one of the many projects sponsored by the Gush Etzion Foundation—the children's shelter in Sde Bar in Gush Etzion.

This shelter is the home to over forty boys at this time, and many more that return there after their army duty is finished, as it is the only home they have. These boys either have no parents, or come from homes where they were abused. The agencies send boys, who no one else can handle, to this shelter, and they have an unbelievable track record in turning these kids around. Just one quantifiable result is that the number of their boys going into elite units in the army is amazing. The home is in need of a learning center, to help these kids make up for all the classes they missed.

Due to the beautiful art that Yakira produced, and to the inspiring choice that she made, she raised over $1,000 today to donate to the Sde Bar home.

⟡

Helping the Israeli Economy

Whenever my dad gives my kids money, he also gives them money to give to charity in amounts of $50 or more. Once my son refused to take any gift money from my dad until my dad insisted and said, "you have to help the Israeli economy." After much nudging my son finally agreed to accept some gift money but rather than going out and buying himself new sneakers or a CD he asked if we could buy some organic grape juice that his friend's family makes to support themselves. This is a family with ten kids that adopted another. The father was a tour guide whose business suffered with the downturn in the Israeli economy. My son chose to spend his gift money to buy grape juice in order to help them. A true act of kindness.

Locks of Kindness

We have been trying to get my eight-year-old daughter to agree to cut her hair because it is hard to manage. But she wasn't prepared to cut her beautiful golden silky hair. She is a bit chubby and overly sensitive about it. Since her hair is her pride and joy, she was not about to part with it.

Two nights ago, my twelve-year-old daughter decided to cut her long hair and donate it to make a wig for a cancer patient through Zichron Menachem, a Jerusalem charity started by a family whose son died of cancer. (They also provide many other wonderful services for kids with cancer.)

We put her hair up into a ponytail, and as I was cutting it off, my younger daughter suddenly decided that she wanted to do the same. When we finished both haircuts, my eight-year-old asked how long it would take before her hair grew back and she could donate another one!

The same girl who was so proud of her gorgeous hair was prouder of what she had done to help someone. She even said she regretted that she could only give to one person. The next day in school, my twelve-year-old told me some of her classmates plan to do the same.

My five-year-old was very proud of his sisters and he told his grandfather on the phone in the U.S. that they cut their hair and gave it to someone called Sartan (the Hebrew word for cancer).

More than a dozen hair donations were made last year in our community, Gush Etzion! Please spread this message to teachers, and hair salons.

What Wonderful Souls They Have

My second-grade daughter couldn't find her water bottle to take to school today. Whenever she forgets it, she comes home extremely upset explaining how thirsty she has been all day without it, so I knew how important it was to her. I saw another bottle on the kitchen counter and I said, "Here, take this, it belongs to *Abba* (Dad)."

She absolutely refused to take it and said that it is not right to have *Abba* go without. I told her that he would somehow manage, but she continued to explain how it would be wrong for her to take his. Even though children can sometimes be self-engrossed, on such occasions like this one, it is inspiring to see what wonderful souls they have!

Teaching Kindness in Schools

I answer questions from teachers that are emailed to me from the Institute of Educational Technology, which works together with the teachers' union.

Yesterday they sent me four letters from teachers at Israeli Arab schools. Although painful, it is important to relate to them. The last letter was the most challenging. A junior high school teacher complained about the violent behavior of a few students and asked what to do about it. I wrote a long letter. I thought about the projects mentioned on the *Daily Dose of Kindness* emails that are implemented in schools, and suggested she start thinking of ways to promote kindness, caring and peace.

✐∻≈≈∻✐

Kindness of Friends

When my daughter wasn't feeling well, and had to be hospitalized, we were able to cope with that anxious time through the kindness of many friends who:

◇ Left work early to bake our daughter's favorite cookies and bring them to the hospital.

◇ Brought her a special scrapbook so she could either use it as a diary, art pad, or album.

◇ Made her a CD of her favorite songs.

◇ Called every day to see if we were okay or if we just wanted to talk.

◇ Offered information and resources that could be helpful to us.

◇ Came over late at night to wash dishes when I had no more energy.

◇ Prayed for her speedy recovery.

We thank God for making our daughter well again and for sending so many friends to help us.

The Apple Doesn't Fall Far from the Tree

An eleven-year-old boy in Jerusalem noticed that his teacher didn't have a watch. And when he finally acquired one, it was a rather inexpensive watch—more like a toy for a child, than something suitable for this boy's FAVORITE teacher!

The child mentioned it to his parents, who suggested that the boy do something about it. He decided to collect money from the other youngsters in the class, and when he had enough (with some help from his parents), he and his father went to pick out a watch for the teacher. The children in the class gave the teacher the watch along with a meaningful hand-written card.

The Tissue That Made My Day

My five-year-old, Chana, had fallen asleep near my bed. It was early in the morning, before sunrise. I got up for a few minutes and then fell back to sleep, sniffling. I needed a tissue but was too tired to get up again to get one, when Chana on her own initiative, got up and walked to the bathroom, and brought me back a tissue! It was so cute and thoughtful that it made my whole day. And I returned the kindness by making sure that she knew how special I thought her gesture was.

⟜⟝⟞⟝⟜

A Special Cake

Several nights ago a neighbor's daughter came running down the stairs to my apartment to ask my advice on a quick way to frost a cake. It was smack in the middle of supper and bedtime, my most pressured time of the day; I was taking care of all my own kids as well as the child of a friend who just had a baby and needed help.

It's hard to do that on one leg while standing at my door with all the children around me, but I tried. Then I closed the door and went back to my hubbub and thought more about the question. "I had all kinds of frostings and equipment out already since I had filled an order for someone earlier on that day for my small cake business; why not tell her to come down after my kids were in bed and I would just quickly do her cake for her also," I thought. So I told her to come back after my kids were in bed.

I had planned on doing a nice but simple job. While I was preparing the board and starting the designing, she explained why she needed the cake at the last minute. The cake was her fifteen-year-old brother's idea; he had called their mother and asked her to quickly bake a cake for a boy in his class who did not have a mother. It was the boy's birthday that night and he had just completed his study of a section of *Talmud* and was going to make a small celebration. After I understood what she said to me, I told her, in that case, we cannot do a simple job; it has to be really nice and honorable looking.

Thank God we got it done on time and it came out very, very nice. It was hard to frost since the cake was too hot and soft to frost and we did not have any time to spare—it had pretty much just come out of the oven. Usually one needs to let a cake cool off first before frosting. It was clearly God's help that got it to come out so nice under the circumstances.

It was a beautiful act of kindness, from many different people, all to make an orphan happy. And it left all of us feeling uplifted and inspired.

⌾᷍᷍᷍᷍᷍᷍⌾

We Have So Much to Learn from these First Graders

First grade is the first time students learn to pray from a *siddur* (prayer book). In order to make this milestone exciting, they often perform a play and have a special "*siddur* party." In my daughter's school in Beit Shemesh there is a first-grade student who suffers from cancer. She has been in and out of the hospital for treatments throughout the year.

It looked like this student would be in the hospital and miss the long-awaited "*siddur* party." The children and teachers put in a lot of effort to make it a spectacular event.

Rather than have her miss this exciting event, the entire class—teacher, principal and musician—went to the hospital and made the *siddur* party there. The students wore beautiful costumes, sang in a choir and performed a play. Afterwards each girl received her first *siddur*, prayer book.

They invited all of the other children from the hospital ward and they enjoyed the performance immensely. It was definitely the most moving *siddur* party I have ever seen!! I wish I could share with you the beautiful pictures which depict the acts of these young girls, being taught the true meaning of loving kindness.

Months later, we received this update to the story:

A few months ago, I shared with you the story of a first-grader in my daughter's school in Beit Shemesh whose class conducted their *siddur* party at the hospital at which she was receiving chemo treatments. I am happy to report that, thank God, she has returned to school and is doing well. When she first returned to school, she wore a wig. Thank God her hair has started growing back and she no longer needs to wear a wig. She has a short-cropped hair cut which will, God willing, grow.

In my daughter's school almost every girl has a long pony tail or braid. This girl would have been the only one in her class without one. So, several students, including her older sister, decided to cut their hair short.

We have so much to learn from these first-graders.

∽ ❦ ∽

First Class First Graders

Hillel, my beautiful first-grade son, was born with a rare blood sugar disorder. Although he looks totally ordinary (yet gorgeous) to the average passerby, he has been through a great deal in his short six-and-a-half-years. His daily routine includes many medications, a special diet and regular finger pricks. He is tracked by several types of specialists, and battles an accompanying eating disorder that complicates everything from going to school to attending birthday parties to visiting friends.

A couple of weeks ago, I received a call from the mother of one of Hillel's classmates. "My son was chosen to be the Student of the Week and he has to bring in a snack for the whole class. He insisted that I call you to find out what Hillel can eat. He only wants me to buy something that everyone, including Hillel, can share," she told me. Has your heart ever broken and soared at the very same time?

When I went into parent-teacher meetings the following week, I related the story to my son's teacher. She told me, with justified pride, that this all started a week earlier, when a different Student of the Week showed up with a special sugar-free snack just for Hillel.

My son Hillel just walked in from school with a bag of chips in his hand and his eyes glowing. For the third week in a row, his class's Student of the Week, a six-year-old first grader, managed to explain to his mother that there is a special boy in his class for whom he would like to do an act of kindness.

There are many people to thank—my son's teacher, who, no doubt, played a great role in both her guidance and responses to the boys' spontaneous acts of kindness; the parents, who listened and understood what their sons were requesting and acted on their requests; but most importantly a special class of first-grade students who reached out and embraced a special little boy.

⌐῎⩓⩓⫯⟋

I'm the One

One day, when I came to fetch my four-year-old from kinder-garten, her teacher pulled me over to the side and related the following episode:

"One of the girls said a pretty bad word and acted very silly. When I told her that I was going to punish her and put her in the corner, she started to cry. Then your daughter came over to me and told me:

'You know, teacher, really you're supposed to put me in the corner, because I'm the one who told her to say that word and act up. So, please, teacher, look she's so sad....'"

The teacher was really impressed.

⌐῎⩓⩓⫯⟋

Who Said "The Younger Generation is Selfish"?

I would like to share a kind deed that my sixteen-year-old son did. I'm very proud of him:

As he was walking back home from school, tired and hun-gry, with his book bag on his shoulder, he saw an old man pushing his wife and their groceries up a hill in a slow moving, two passenger, electric vehicle. The man was having a very hard time pushing. He explained to my son that the battery was dead and that's why he had to push.

"Climb in and sit down," my son told him as he pushed the

couple and their groceries up the hill and took them all the way to their home.

The man and his wife, who were Russian immigrants, couldn't stop thanking him.

I can't stop smiling when I think of this special, kind act. Who said "The younger generation is selfish"?

The Bride and Her Happy Campers

I have two girls, ages ten and thirteen, who have Down's Syndrome. For the past two summers they have gone to an overnight camp run by Ezer Mizion. Batya, my thirteen-year-old, had the same counselor for both years. Lala, as the girls call her, really loved her campers. She even called last summer to make sure Batya was coming back to camp.

Lala got married about a month ago in Jerusalem. She sent Batya an invitation and wanted her to come so much that she had a friend call us to make sure that Batya would come. Since we live in a small community north of Jerusalem, we told her friend that it would not be possible for my daughter to go because there were no buses back to our community at that time of night. So Lala had her friend ask her mother if Batya could sleep at their house the night after the wedding.

The friend picked my daughter up from school and brought her to school the next day. Batya had a great time. She even danced with the bride.

It just totally amazes me that on one of the most important

days of her life that Lala should be so concerned that my daughter attends.

Batya passed away at age fourteen, less than a year after this story took place.

Fun Little People

A couple who live in an apartment across the hall from us had their first baby a few months ago. It has been a major adjustment for the new mother. As many new mothers realize right away, a first baby is actually more time consuming and difficult than they imagined.

Suddenly, going out to the corner store to buy milk, fixing a meal, cleaning the house, or just simply taking a shower can be overwhelming, when "little lady" decides to scream or fuss for hours on end, unless, of course, she is being held.

Thank God, we have three children who are still young, though not so small anymore. So when my neighbor needs a shower or wants to straighten up a bit and has no one to entertain her baby, fun little people—ages four to eight—can be just the thing that's needed. I have assured her over and over how much my kids benefit from her baby, and how she would benefit by letting them watch the baby so she can finish the dishes while they all play within view.

My kids go over all the time, any time she asks for them, and other times as well. She feels comfortable calling or knocking on our door to request them when her baby is fussing. It makes everyone happy all around. So this is really a three-way act of kindness—it makes my children feel important and happy, it makes her baby feel loved and calm, and it strengthens our great friendship.

Although this neighbor has a very cute baby, she does not have a camera to take pictures. So I go over there with our digital camera every few days and snap away, then I put the photos on a CD and—voilà!—she has great shots for her and her husband and both sets of grandparents, with no fee or investment in a camera!

A True Ascent
By Chava Dumas

Our family had spent a lovely day at Avnei Etan, a community in the Golan. In the afternoon we went on a scenic excursion to the Shahor Falls. Since we had done this trek in previous years, we were familiar with the difficulty involved in the climb. After stashing our stroller full of supplies, we began cautiously climbing down the rocky, steep descent into the *wadi* (valley) below. I was trying to walk carefully while tightly clutching the hands of two of our children. My husband was in the rear, watching that no one went too close to the cliff's edge.

We descended lower and lower until we were about to enter an area of overhanging grape vines and olive trees. As we approached, I heard in front of us the distinct sound of a person having difficulty speaking, and the loud, excited ruckus of a large group of people surrounding him.

We all moved aside so my husband could rush ahead of us to see what was happening. Then we followed close behind.

When we arrived in the clearing, we saw in front of us a stunning scene. There was, indeed, a heavy young man exerting much effort to pronounce a blessing before drinking a cup of cold water. He was sitting in a wheelchair, surrounded by at least twenty yeshiva boys who were patiently waiting for their friend to finish enunciating his blessing before they all enthusiastically shouted "AMEN!"

The young men, who were about nineteen years old, explained that everything was OK, that they'd "simply" been carrying their friend along the *wadi* trail and now they were just stopping to rest before their final ascent back up to Avnei Etan.

We were speechless.

Their faces were radiant with the immense joy they felt at their accomplishment. They had succeeded in sharing an experience with their wheelchair-bound friend, who could never in his life have gone hiking in the hills of Israel, or anywhere else for that matter. Their skin was glistening with the sweat they had exerted on behalf of their fellow student, their brother, their friend. The awesome love for their classmate, apparent under that modest canopy of foliage, was palpable, and I felt my eyes moisten. We were so overcome in fact, that we didn't think to ask them the name of their yeshiva. But if this is how the students behaved during their vacation from school, imagine how they were all year round?!

As we parted ways and continued along the trail, we periodically looked up to watch with amazement, as the boys triumphantly continued their ascent. A true ascent of awesome proportion.

Feeling for Others

∼🙐🙐🙐∼

In The Ways of Abraham
By Avraham Ellis

The word *gemach* is an acronym for the Hebrew words meaning acts of loving kindness. Thousands of *gemachs*, organizations devoted to assisting people, exist around the globe, wherever Jewish communities may be found. There are *gemachs* that lend out basic necessities like food, baby supplies, various appliances, or basic services through volunteer work like baby sitting, counseling, or household repairs. There are various catering *gemachs*, baby pacifier *gemachs*, matchmaking, psychological and pastoral *gemachs*. I recently heard about a *gemach* in Jerusalem for people with insomnia; they provide music tapes and various electronic devices for suffering insomniacs.

Opening Motivations

Opening up a *gemach* has at least three prerequisites: the finances to back it, the dedication to keep it running, and the wherewithal to advertise the service. I had a slight problem. I am a dairy farmer on Moshav Yesodot—a small, ninety-family, successful farm settlement in Israel; by no means the typical place to open up a *gemach*, especially a new one. I did not have public relations or money. All I had to work with was the stamina, desire and dedication to properly run a *gemach*.

I prayed for ideas and God answered. One day I concentrated on my telephone. Here I am, in farm country in the Holy

Land, away from the rest of the civilized world, but only a telephone call away from anyone on the globe. Hidden away in my office was an old answering machine. Then it hit me: Combine the two for "Tele*gemach*—the Information *gemach*." The idea is simple and inexpensive, but the results are priceless.

People call in about everything under the sun—from employment needs to match-making, lost-and-found to counseling—organizations and individuals needing volunteers—buyers and sellers of apartments and furniture. I leave the answering machine on from 11:00 p.m. to 7:00 a.m. and during the day I listen to the tape, jot down crucial information, and make connections. I look through magazines and newspapers for interesting job opportunities, items for sale, and so on, to help my callers.

A One-Year's Legacy of Benefits

Although the *gemach* is hardly a year old, it already boasts a host of heart-warming incidents.

A man in the Tel Aviv area offered to donate several beds. I put him in touch with a family of refugees from Iran. He decided to deliver the beds himself. When he arrived at their apartment in Bnei Brak, he found the family sleeping on sheets spread out on the floor. He was so delighted to ease their misery that he called to thank me for enabling him to do a mitzvah.

A widow in Haifa with two sick daughters called about a number of items she needed. I was able to help her by connecting her to a bank clerk who had called to donate a large sum to a needy family, a woman who had called to give away a washing machine, and others. The woman called back, her voice quivering with emotion, to tell me that she had thought that she had no one to turn to in this world, no friends or family—but now I am her family.

There are unfortunately a large number of people with no one to turn to, with difficulties they are too afraid or embarrassed to discuss with others. Many of these people turn to Tele*gemach* because of its anonymous nature. Some call and refuse to give a name or address, and I accept them warmly. I only need their telephone number to get back to them with help. A number of people have contacted me with marital and psychological problems. At times, I have had to do a little research to refer them to the right address. Of course, because the *gemach* itself puts me in touch with so many interesting and kind-hearted people, research is never too difficult, no matter what the issue. I try not to get too emotionally involved with the people who call, to insure that the *gemach* runs smoothly without interfering too much with my personal life or my efforts to help as many people as I can, as quickly as possible.

Calls come in continuously from people who want to get involved in doing acts of kindness. A writer in Tel Aviv, for example, called to request an opportunity to do volunteer work on Fridays. I put him in touch with a widower in his area who had a number of young children, one of them mentally retarded. He had asked for volunteers to take care of this child to allow him to rest and work. Two people living in the same area were able to fill each other's need, but had no idea of the other's existence.

Today, information can be more valuable than money. Companies—entire industries—deal with information. There is no reason why information should not be used in the framework of kindness as well. Vital information exists on a wide scale. The more this data can be condensed into one repository, accessible by all, the more people can be helped by it.

Imagine a network of Tele*gemach* branches set up throughout the world, whereby all cities will be interconnected. Whether it is medical assistance, business opportunities, a date, or another heart-to-heart talk, the individual in need will have an address to turn to.

Edited and adapted by Devora Segall with permission from "The Jewish Observer."

―――

Showing the Ropes to Newcomers

When I moved to Israel there were so many things I didn't know: where to buy what, what *gemachs* there were, where the libraries were and their hours, etc. So by the time a friend moved here I had made a list and gave it to her. I now do that for all newcomers and the list has grown considerably. People appreciate it so much and it really helps the newcomer feel welcome too!

～〰〰〰〰〜

More Than Money

Many times when I walk down the streets of the Old City of Jerusalem, or I walk around Ben Yehudah Street, poor people come over with their hands stretched out asking for charity.

The other day, when I was walking with a friend, a poor lady approached us. Before she even said anything, I saw my friend quickly take out a salad from her bag and give it to the poor lady. The lady kept thanking her. As we walked away, I looked back for a moment and saw her eating the salad with a great big smile on her face. I just couldn't help but think about how happy this small act had made the lady feel and how much more this meant to her than the spare change that most people give.

On another occasion, I was walking down a street in the Old City, on my way to the Western Wall when something extraordinary caught my eye. I saw a poor lady on the side of the street asking for money. Suddenly, a girl went over, and spoke to her briefly. Then the girl did the most amazing thing—she sat there and gave the woman a massage on her shoulders. As she gave the massage, the poor lady was smiling and chuckling and just ecstatic. This too seemed to mean so much more to the poor lady than a few coins.

⸎

Love Between Beggars

As I was walking on Jaffa Street, in Jerusalem, one afternoon, I passed two beggars. One was sitting towards the beginning of the block—he was sleeping, and had very few coins in his hat. The other was sitting towards the end, playing an instrument of some sort, and had many coins in his hat.

I went into a store, and when I came out some time later, I witnessed the most amazing thing: the beggar with many coins scooped up some of his earnings, walked over to the other beggar, and deposited them into that one's hat. Then he sat down by his friend and started talking with him....

⸎

Whose Money is It, Anyway?

I inherited a nice amount of money about a year ago, after my father's death. My first thoughts about what to do with the money were to buy a larger apartment, since we have three children in a two-bedroom apartment. Or maybe we could use it to buy a newer and larger car or for a trip for all of us to visit my family in Europe.

Despite all the thoughts of what we could do with the money, it wound up just sitting in our bank account earning a little bit of interest and doing nothing. Then, one day, my husband told me about one of his cousins, who just had another baby and had not been paid his salary for over half a year. The bank kept giving him more loans every time he asked, until one day, when they told him "That's it, no more, if you don't pay by next week we will take away your apartment."

My husband asked me if I would agree to give his cousin all of the money that we got, as a loan, to be repaid "whenever." At first the "whenever" bothered me a lot—not that I didn't want to help—I like to help whenever I can, but I was a little afraid that we might not get the money back.

I thought over the situation and kept on thinking, "whose money is it, anyway? We didn't earn it; it was just a present. And even if we had worked to earn it, it's just material. What would we do with it? Buy a bigger apartment, a better car, and more clothes or just let it sit in the bank, to the bank's benefit?"

I "fought" with myself for a few moments, and decided that we had no use for the money at the moment anyway, it was just sitting there, and now we had the opportunity to "help the needy." So I told my husband that I would love to give his cousin the money.

Going the Extra Mile

I live in a community in YESHA (Judea, Samaria and Gaza) and the people here are great! Everyone is very community minded and helpful.

One Saturday night, I had planned to make a going away party for a family that was moving to Jerusalem. To my surprise, it fell on exactly the same evening my husband and I were expected to attend a *bar mitzvah* dinner held about a block away.

We had to be in two places at once, so we decided to make the going away party a bit earlier than the dinner, and hoped to leave the party we made early, and arrive to the dinner a little late—something that many in Israel do anyway.

After saying goodbye to my guests (a really awkward situation) I told them they were all invited to still stay at my house and enjoy themselves, and that we would be back as soon as we could. We arrived home about 10:30 p.m. hoping we would still catch the last of our guests, and then I and my husband would clean up after a long evening. The guests had all recently left when we returned, but the house was clean! All the party dishes and food were put away, the floor was swept, and there was nothing to do, but fall into bed in blissful sleep.

I really want to thank the family that stayed and cleaned up. They could have just left, but they went that extra mile. It was so kind and thoughtful, and I was really touched. I always try to teach my own children that anyone can do what they are told, but going that "extra" mile, doing over and above, THAT is real kindness.

Thanks to all of you who do that extra something that is not expected. It makes the world so much nicer and kinder!

⟊⟊⟊

More than the Money

I witnessed the following incident in a supermarket in Ramat Beit Shemesh:

A woman was waiting in line with her children at the check-out counter. She was standing behind a twelve-year-old girl who clearly had been sent to the store by her mother to pick up a few items. It turned out that the girl was a few shekels short of the amount she needed.

As the girl tried to decide what to put back, the woman behind her, who knew how frustrating it was to have to put something back because you are missing a small amount of money, quickly handed her the money she needed.

What impressed me even more than the small amount of money she gave, were the kind words she included afterwards. Many people would rather part with a couple of shekels instead of having to stand longer on a line with impatient children, waiting for the cashier to undo the transaction—but as she handed the girl the money, she made sure to tell her, "You can give the money to charity when you get home."

This thoughtful comment was meant to spare the girl embarrassment. The woman was reassuring her and was really telling her, "I know the problem is not that you cannot afford the groceries, but just that you got stuck AND do not be embarrassed to accept the money from me because I am really donating it to charity—not to you."

Just in case the girl still felt embarrassed in any way, the woman also made sure to add, "It happens to me all the time...."

Everything She Does for All of Us

Many of us are familiar with the typical mother-in-law and daughter-in-law tensions. Tonight I was at a fiftieth birthday party of a divorced friend of mine. Her two daughters-in-law (with the help of her two married sons, and three other kids) made the party for her—they cooked and made a fabulous event down to every last detail and wouldn't accept help from anyone.

One daughter-in-law who had a baby about a month before the party, and still worked tirelessly to help, got up to speak and said:

"B. forbade me to speak about her, so I'll abide by her request, reluctantly, but I just must say that this party we made for her is NOTHING at all in comparison to everything she does for all of us on a daily basis—for all of us, her kids, her grandchildren—everyone. We are eternally grateful to her."

It was so touching. Even though my friend is divorced, she is a very happy and fulfilled person to have such a wonderful relationship, not only with her kids, but more remarkably, with her two daughters-in-law. In fact, she just redid her basement to earn some extra income as a small rental apartment. Her son and daughter-in-law asked if they could rent it! The daughter-in-law was only too thrilled to live in the same house as her mother-in-law, and of course my friend is thrilled to have them, and her two grandchildren live practically under the same roof.

∽╫╫╫╨∾

The Best Surprise

Whenever I meet someone who is in the dumps, I ask them to tell me about the best surprise they ever had. Even though I tell them that it does not have to be a happy event, I have never heard anyone relate a sad surprise. They always talk about happy surprises.

This technique can help a person to relive their happy memories. Just remembering and relating a memorable event puts someone into a completely different frame of mind. It works with everyone. You can even try it even with someone who is already happy.

∽╫╫╫╨∾

The "New" Couch

Friends of ours don't have it so easy financially—the father is a teacher and they have nine kids. Recently their twenty-year-old couch completely broke apart. They were looking to buy a used one since a new couch wasn't in their budget.

When I saw an email offer to give away an old couch, I replied in their name, but it was already taken—free offers go quickly around here (in Israel).

This morning, I saw another such email just as it came in, so I replied immediately in their name. Then I called them up and told them to claim it right away in person. Thank God they got it. Now they finally have a place to sit.

While they were clearing up the area in order to move in their "new" couch, they found a book that my daughter needed for school. I couldn't find the book in the bookstore, and no one on our email list had it.

They remembered my email about the book and let me know they had it. When my daughter went to pick it up, they told her how they found it—all because of moving in the "new" couch.

My daughter came home all excited when she saw an example of something that she had learned about many times: "one *mitzvah* leads to another."

⌁≈∽

Sometimes All It Takes Is a Few Phone Calls

I was able to make a few quick phone calls to bring comfort to a close friend.

My friend and her family have a hard life. She has four children, one of whom is a thirteen-year-old girl with special needs. The family's financial situation is severe.

Recently she was suffering from both an excruciatingly painful slipped disc in her back, and also a neurological condition which has caused loss of muscle control in her neck. The condition is only treatable to a certain extent and may well be irreversible. She's been in the hospital for weeks, and has just come home.

After making a few phone calls to charity funds, I found one that agreed to pay for new beds with orthopedic mattresses for the couple, something that will hopefully alleviate the back pain. The beds arrived the next day.

My friend did not have a comfortable chair to sit on, so I made one more phone call to a wealthy relative of hers, who was happy to buy one for her. The chair arrived as promised.

Sometimes all it takes is a few phone calls to alleviate so much suffering.

⁓✦⁓

We All Do Make a Difference in the World

I work in the community of Bet El. The only access road to Bet El is through an Israeli army base.

Each morning when I drive to work and have to pass through the gate/checkpoint, I always, thank the soldiers on guard duty there and say, *"Todah al hashmira"* which roughly means, "Thanks for guarding us." Since there are many different soldiers on duty there all the time, I am not really familiar with any of them.

Every time I pass the checkpoint, I keep thinking that these soldiers have to stand by the checkpoint in the heat of summer when the sun beats down on them and also in the winter when they are bundled up, freezing in the cold rain and wind. Sometimes when I thank them for guarding us all, I wonder if they think I am a strange person for doing so, or even laugh to themselves about this lady who drives in and always thanks them. One day I learned the answer to my question in such a beautiful way....

One cold day while driving home, I picked up some hitch-hikers to take them to another community. One of the hitchhik-ers was a soldier. He smiled when he entered my car and thanked me for picking him up and giving him a ride. I told him that it was my pleasure to help him out.

When we got to our destination he asked me where I was turning so he could get out and walk a few blocks to his home. I asked him what street he lived on, since it was very cold and wet that day, and I wanted to drop him off in front of his home.

He said, "Oh no, you can let me walk. I don't want to make you go out of your way."

I explained to him that I was in a car, so it made no differ-ence to me to go a bit further, but if he had to walk, it would be much harder for him. And so, reluctantly, he told me where to turn to get to his street.

After bringing him to his house, the soldier again profusely thanked me, and I just told him, "No, I thank YOU, since you are always guarding our people and the Land of Israel."

He smiled and said to me: "I wish everyone was like you. When you drive into Bet El, you always thank us for our guard-ing!"

Well, needless to say, when the soldier got out of the car and waved goodbye to me with a big smile, I felt like a full circle had closed. I had gotten my answer.

My constant "thank you's" were not being laughed at; rather, the soldiers really did appreciate them.

It brought tears to my eyes, and reminded me that although we don't always merit t see the results of our actions, we all do make a difference in the world. And sometimes we are even lucky enough to see it for ourselves!

This One-Minute Conversation Made His Day

In my synagogue in Israel, I noticed that a young Ethiopian boy had begun coming by himself to morning and evening services. Today I introduced myself and offered to help him, since his family only recently moved to the area. His smile was very genuine. Our one-minute conversation made his day.

Kindness Meter

I parked my car on a street near the center of Jerusalem. After I put money into the meter I noticed that the meter of the car parked next to me had expired. I looked up the street and noticed a policeman walking in my direction, giving out tickets to cars whose meters had expired. So I dug into my wallet and found a five-shekel ($1.25) coin and dropped it into the meter of the car next to mine.

∼⊱⊰∼

Reach Out to Friends and Strangers

I was once sitting in Ben Gurion airport, waiting for my flight to be announced. Suddenly I heard a strange, almost animal-like noise. I looked around and realized that a woman sitting a few rows in front of me was weeping loudly.

I was a little thrown and did not know what to do. Should I allow her privacy? Should I approach her? My heart went out to her, crying alone in an airport.

An older woman, who had also noticed her, went up to her and said something, but then moved away again and I guessed that she had refused an offer of help. She continued with her aching crying, and I continued to wonder if I should do something nonetheless.

Eventually I plucked up my courage and went over. Rather than ask if everything was OK, which would probably have elicited a polite rebuttal as in the case of the other woman, I sat down next to her and said (I don't recall my exact words), "I don't want to intrude on your privacy, but I couldn't help noticing that you are in distress."

I guess she saw the genuine empathy in my eyes, as she proceeded to pour out her story. Her sister, who was relatively young, had just lost her husband, and this woman had spent the week being the rock upon which her sister could lean. Only now that she was leaving did she allow the flood of grief for her sister to deluge her, to the point where she abandoned her inhibitions and bawled her heart out in such a public place.

She spoke to me for a just a few minutes, but I sensed that she parted from me a little comforted; for somebody else had just for a moment reached out to her and provided a shoulder for her to cry on, in a reversal of her usual role.

I am often afraid of rejection and assume that no one would want me specifically to comfort them. But it's not true—where there is real emotion, there can never be enough warm hands to hold, empathetic eyes to reflect the pain, and shoulders to cry on.

⚓

Oh, Bother! Another Unsolicited Email That I Really Don't Need

I just wanted you to know the positive effect that receiving your weekly emails has been having on me.

Initially, when I first received the emails, I thought, "Oh, bother, another unsolicited email that I really don't need." I thought of sending an email to cancel but then I thought, "What kind of person am I if I cancel an email that helps people to become more kind?"

So each week I read them and find them really down-to-earth and at the same time inspiring. But more than that, I find that the simple but crucial lessons that are embedded in the little anecdotes are gradually seeping into my behavior. I recall them when I pass a beggar on the street or volunteer to help strangers find their way around Jerusalem. It's heightening my awareness of the "little things" one can do to reach out to others, and that is very meaningful.

So thank you for doing what you are doing.

∼⁂∼

They Liked It

I gave a series of classes on baking and dessert making. Even though I know I gave out great recipes and that the tips I shared with all the women were good ones, nevertheless, one never really knows if the people are satisfied or if they think the class was worth their time and money. It can be a bit nerve-racking at times, not knowing if it's really going over well.

At the end of the second class, and even more so at the end of the last class, several of the ladies came over to me and wholeheartedly told me how much they liked what I taught and how much they truly enjoyed their time with me.

They need not have said what they did. They had paid me and I would probably not see most of them again, since they didn't live in my neighborhood. But it so much made my day and gave me such a boost of confidence—it was a tremendous act of kindness for me. Furthermore, it made such a difference to me that I may very well give more classes next month just because of what they said!

The Workers Caught Me

At my health club in Tel Aviv they provide a minimum of two towels to each member. The cleaning attendants in the locker room works very hard, but unfortunately they are not appreciated by everyone. Some women leave their towels just anywhere instead of putting them in the designated bins.

I make it a point to not only bring my own towels to the bins, but to visually scour the locker room before I leave and take all the towels left on the floor, alleviating the work load just a bit for the women who are already doing a lot of physical work.

At least once, when the workers "caught" me, I saw how good it made them feel to see that someone appreciated their labors.

It "Pays" to Help

When the Bank of Israel introduced a new 50-NIS ($13) bill, all vendors accepted both the old and the new bill for some months thereafter. When, finally, stores stopped accepting the old ones you could only make the exchange at the bank.

Shortly after the cutoff date, I took the afternoon off to be with my youngest daughter. As a treat I took her to the kosher fast food place for some french fries. Since it was lunchtime and the place was busy, people became restless because of long lines. When I finally decided to see what was taking so long I discovered that two children had ordered lunch and were trying to pay with an old 50-NIS bill. It was all the money that they had and the attendant would not accept it. Neither would the manager. She kept trying to explain to the children that they had to go to the bank (which was closed for lunch) exchange the bill and come back for their lunch. Everybody was starting to make a fuss and the older child just didn't know what to do.

I checked my wallet and saw that I had a new 50-NIS bill and exchanged it with the boy. I would exchange the old 50-NIS for a new bill the next time I went to the bank. It was so simple. And it should have ended there....

That night I had to go out. As I was walking home I remembered that there was supposed to be an eclipse. So I walked most of the way home looking up at the moon. As I turned the corner to my street I decided that I had seen enough and should watch where I am going. There on the ground I found another new 50-NIS bill.

∽⧼⧽⧽∾

Driving Our Teacher
By Rachel Hershberg

Our wonderful nursery school teacher's car was stolen, and she was forced to take a taxi to both drop off her own kids and get to work. I'm sure that even before this added expense, she was not making a salary that was commensurate with the importance of her work.

After half an hour of phone calls I had set up a rotation of parents to bring her to kindergarten and her kids to their school and then return them in the afternoon. Everyone was eager to help.

∽⧼⧽⧽∾

What a Great Way to Help Out My Late Friend!

A few weeks ago, I needed to remove a bed from our storage room in order to make room for our new freezer. I tried to sell it, but to no avail.

Then a neighbor told me that there was a poor family that could use the bed. It turned out to be the family of my best friend who was killed in a car accident three years previously. Her husband has not yet remarried. He has four young children and very little money to buy any real furniture. My friend's eleven-year-old daughter did not have a proper bed.

I found and paid for a mover so that they would not have any expenses from it at all. The young girl really enjoys her new bed.

What a great way to help out my late friend!

❦

No Way to Express the Wonders of This Community

We just made *aliyah*—moved to Israel. I feel I just have to share our first experiences in a small way to show the great appreciation we have for the Beit Shemesh community on Rechov Gad and the surrounding neighborhoods.

First of all, we must thank the amazing organization, Nefesh b'Nefesh, for really helping make our dream of *aliyah* a reality.

Secondly, we have to thank a realtor named Shelly, for getting us an apartment without a real deposit and allowing us to move in immediately upon our arrival at around midnight.

Shelly told us the community was amazing and she was so right. From the very first night we arrived, our new neighbors, one couple from Australia and one family from America, helped get the keys to get us in and gave us food and offered so much more. We later found out that they had posted an email about us on the Beit Shemesh email list.

The next morning we awoke feeling happy to be here but overwhelmed and unsure how to get breakfast for our kids. A few minutes later there was a knock on the door. A neighbor introduced herself and handed us a bag filled with cereal, milk, bowls and spoons. Later that day another neighbor brought over a table and chairs. We also received from other neighbors a love-seat, a burner and many cooked meals. Mattresses were offered, but we actually brought some air mattresses with us from America.

We have been invited over for nearly every Sabbath dinner and lunch, since we arrived. The American family we met the first night also lent us their cell phone the first few days. They and other neighbors let us use their Internet connections, have given us rides and one neighbor showed up with a hamper to do our laundry.

People we do not know actually walk up to us and, realizing we are new in town, introduce themselves and offer assistance. There is no sufficient way to express how unbelievably amazing this community is.

One of our Australian neighbors, who helped me a great deal, told me of the time her brother was in the hospital in Jerusalem. Although she did not have a car, she wanted to visit him every day.

The community, without her knowing, arranged to have someone tell her everyday they were going to Jerusalem, and would offer her a ride. Then when visiting hours were over, someone else would call her on her cell phone to tell her they were in the area and they just wanted to see if she needed a ride home.

We now, thank God, have many new friends that I truly hope to remain friends with for many years, from America, Australia, England, South Africa and of course Israel. We can never thank them enough for all they have done, but we do pray that we will be able to help many new immigrants in the future. We also pray that there are or that there will be, many more communities like this one.

⟪✦⟫

"Strangers?" No, Not Really

One fine summer morning during vacation, a mother with eight children called a van service to take them to the zoo in Jerusalem.

There was always plenty to see and do in this lovely, landscaped location, to keep children of all ages busily enthused. The father of the family was able to meet up with them later in the afternoon. Once they were all united, they decided to split up into three groups to cover more territory. Then they wandered off in different directions with a plan to meet back together at 7 p.m., when the zoo closed. Some children went with their father to see the penguins, several went with their mother to see the lemurs, and a few more went with their oldest sibling to watch the elephant feeding.

Amazingly, at the appointed time, they all managed to meet at the designated place. They called the driver of the van who had originally brought them earlier in the day, and arranged to have him pick them up in half an hour.

They heard the announcement that the zoo was officially closed, and all the visitors had to clear out. Amidst the huge throng of departing visitors, the family successfully maneuvered to the other side of the entrance gate to wait for their hired van to arrive.

By now, the children were very tired and hungry after their seven-hour expedition. They were whining and anxious to get home. Surrounded by the sea of humanity swarming out, it was a real scene! Every time another large vehicle pulled in to the pick up area, it was enveloped by people who all urgently needed a ride. The sky was gradually growing darker and their van still hadn't shown up.

There was nothing to do but sit and wait patiently. The mother, who knew what their driver looked like, stood by the curb, peering worriedly in the window of each newly arriving van. It seemed as though he would never show up!

After a forty-five minute wait, she finally spotted him. Overcome with relief, exhausted and happy to actually be heading home, they all unceremoniously clambered in and found places to sit. The littlest ones immediately fell asleep.

Too tired to speak, the twenty-five-minute drive passed uneventfully. Just as they neared the approach to the turn off to their neighborhood in northern Jerusalem, the oldest child's voice was heard, nervously asking, "Mommy, where is Bracha?"

"What do you mean, where is Bracha? She's sleeping next to Daddy!" her mother quickly replied.

"No, she's not!" Sarah answered.

"Daddy!! Isn't Bracha sleeping next to you?" The mother asked in disbelief.

"No, I thought she was with you!"

"What do you mean...? She was never next to me! I thought she was next to you all this time! I thought she was asleep! Where is she?!"

They all started looking under the seats, shouting, "Bracha! Bracha!" in hopes that she
would wake up and say something!

Stunned, they suddenly realized there was no Bracha in the van anywhere!

"When was the last time anyone saw her," the mother sobbed. "Didn't she get in with us?"

She shouted to the driver, "Turn around! Turn around! We have to go back to the zoo immediately!"

The driver swung his head, "What? What?"

"Our five-year-old daughter isn't here! We have to go back!"

So right there at the intersection, when they were nearly home, he made a U-turn and zoomed back in the direction from which they just came, while the mother frantically searched through her bag for their yearly pass, on which was printed the zoo's telephone number. When she found it, she couldn't read the numbers in the dark, so the driver told her to give it to him. He read aloud while she tensely pressed the numbers on her cell phone. It was late and the zoo had closed over an hour earlier. Who would be there now? Who would answer?

"I can't believe this! I can't believe we forgot her! How could we not notice!? Where is she?!"

"Calm down, you are scaring everyone," her husband implored.

"Ah! How can I calm down!" The phone kept ringing and ringing. Finally—someone answered!

"Hello! Did you find a lost child?" She wailed. "A five-year-old. No? You don't have her?" In her fright, she couldn't get any more Hebrew words to come out coherently.

The driver insisted, "Give me the phone!"

He shouted excitedly into the receiver and they all waited tensely for a response.

"She went to look!" He told them. The lone person left in the zoo office was searching for their missing child in the premises outside the gates.

Four more horrible minutes passed with the driver holding the phone, speeding down the highway, before he announced,

"They found her!"

At 8:45 p.m., an hour after they'd left, they arrived at a zoo that was completely dark and deserted. There on a stone bench, sitting beside the petunia blossoms, quietly sucking her thumb, was their precious Bracha. She was sitting with a family.

They must have also been a tired, hungry family, anxious to head home and feed their restless youngsters and get them into bed. They also had a long way to travel. Yet there they were just sitting and waiting for over an hour, with a little five-year-old who wouldn't say a word about who she was or what her phone number was, or where she lived. They were just sitting and waiting with her until her family finally came, so she wouldn't feel abandoned and afraid. So she would feel safe.

Bracha's Dad jumped out, scooped her up, and profusely thanked the couple for their tremendously appreciated kindness. Was it possible to adequately thank them enough for their good deed of kind consideration towards a young unknown child?

He carried Bracha into the van, where her siblings immediately surrounded and hugged her. They all cried with relief to have her safe with them again. Even the toddler kissed her on the head.

They all realized, with immense gratitude, how important it was that people—"strangers"—were willing to go out of their way to wait and watch their lost loved one. "Strangers?" No, not really.

Medical
Issues

An Honor to Be Part of Such a People

Once again, we were the recipients of countless acts of kindness during our son's recent hospitalization. What a beautiful moment, when a young girl came to the pediatric ward accompanied by her father. An older woman explained that today was the girl's *bat mitzvah*, and she chose to spend the day giving out bags of "goodies" to patients in the hospital. My son had recently regained his appetite, and was more than happy to partake. The bag was generous enough that when we returned home there was enough to give to his siblings.

How warming it was to see seminary girls use their free time, to dress up like clowns, and to come in to the rooms to shape balloons, blow bubbles, and exude warmth and caring.

How truly healing it was to see a grown man (clearly a professional clown) take the time to make the mothers laugh along with their children.

I never had to worry about what I would eat when I was visiting my son in the hospital. Ezer Mizion delivered a fresh hot meal every day with a smile and heartfelt blessings for his speedy and complete recovery.

But what about my family at home? Never fear, for *Klal Yisroel*—the Community of Israel—was always there—early morning, lunch time and evenings. Seminary students came to help get the kids out, clean up, fold laundry, iron, run errands, straighten up—whatever was needed.

It is only more poignant to add that these students were adult women, many of whom have professions which they had put on hold to come to Israel to strengthen themselves in their

Torah observance and to learn about the religion they never had the opportunity to experience as children.

Neighbors, many of whom with large families of their own, and sometimes a kid or two at home with one winter ailment or another, nonetheless managed to send meals to my not-small family. It is truly an honor to be part of such a people.

─✦─

Delicious Deeds
By C.K., Jerusalem

I had heard about Ezer Mizion and their various kindness projects at local Jerusalem hospitals. "That's nice for people who are sick," I thought. "Lucky I don't need their good deeds." But it seems that I spoke too soon.

My first personal encounter with Ezer Mizion was while my husband and I were in the waiting room of a hospital's emergency room. I sensed someone standing nearby and as I looked up I saw a friendly hand extending two neatly wrapped sweet rolls. Needless to say, the sweet rolls were more than welcome and we gladly accepted.

Many hours later, as I was assisting my husband with his food tray, again I looked up to see a friendly hand this time offering me a neatly wrapped sandwich. I hadn't even realized that I was hungry until I saw the sandwich. I gratefully accepted.

A few weeks later I was in a room with other people waiting to hear when our relative would be out of the operating room.

Again I felt a friendly presence and I looked up again to see a friendly hand offering a neatly wrapped sandwich.

Although the food was more than welcome, the kindness and concern of these volunteers from Ezer Mizion was the greatest kindness of all. I was truly blessed to receive their kindness.

⟡

Gratitude
By Rachel Hershberg

My daughter was just in the hospital for four days with a skin infection on her forehead. After getting over the initial shock and fear of the first few days, I began to feel tremendous gratitude to so many.

I am thankful to the Creator for providing Israel with advanced medicine and antibiotics and of course, for my daughter's recovery.

I am also grateful to my husband. Because I have a nursing baby I couldn't stay overnight in the hospital so my husband spent the bulk of the time in the hospital with our daughter making what could have been a traumatic experience for our daughter, into a fun and special time with dad.

Also, I am grateful to my friends who went out of their way to give me a ride into Jerusalem, took care of my other kids, left dinner in front of my door one night, bought us food for the Sabbath, brought by a dessert, and generally provided technical and emotional support.

I am also grateful to my family, who called and expressed love and concern.

I am extremely grateful to the staff—doctors, nurses, cleaning staff, everyone at Shaarei Tzedek Hospital who took such good care of my daughter, and did their best to treat us as human beings.

Lastly, I must make special mention of the volunteers at Shaarei Tzedek. My daughter's meals were served by young women doing their year of National Service; her art projects were supervised by immigrants from France and the US. Two students in Israel for a year cheered us all up as clowns; someone came by everyday with meals for the parents of the sick kids from the organization Ezer Mizion. (Gratitude must be expressed also to those who donated money to pay for those meals.)

I am deeply inspired by all of these kindnesses.

The New Father Who Had Kindness to Spare
By C.K., Jerusalem

It was a hot Jerusalem summer afternoon. My husband was a bit weak having just been discharged from a large Jerusalem hospital. We arrived at our car in the parking lot to find that it had a flat tire. A gentleman was returning to his car near by and we asked if he knew any local gas station that would come to change a tire. He replied that he did not know of any local station, but he would be glad to change the tire for us!

The gentleman refused to accept any payment from us. Then he proceeded to invite us to his son's circumcision! Apparently he had just been visiting with his wife and their new baby in the hospital.

We felt honored to receive this gentleman's act of kindness and also to be invited to share his celebration. How lucky is the baby boy to have a father like this—great both in honor and in charity!

⌐᷐᷎᷏᷌᷍⌐

Hospital Filled with Kindness

My husband, who is eighty-one years old, felt dizzy and almost fell while walking home from synagogue on Friday. A team of medics advised us to go to Jerusalem's Shaarei Tzedek Hospital immediately.

His heartbeat was irregular, his pulse and blood pressure were way down. I was worried about his condition and also about how we would get through the Sabbath at the hospital.

As soon as we arrived, the hospital staff began treating him. After a few hours his condition improved. The kind acts that were done for us during his hospital stay were overwhelming.

When an Arab technician finished monitoring my husband's lungs, he brought us a copy of the English edition of the newspaper *Hamodia*; he told us that the emergency room receives two copies. What kindness and thoughtfulness on his part (and on the hospital's part). Although we subscribe to *Hamodia*, it never occurred to me to grab our copy on our speedy exit from home. It gave me a taste of home.

Later I asked for some food for my husband, since he hadn't made *kiddush*—the Friday night blessing on a cup of wine, or eaten. It was after regular eating hours, but the attendants found a meal for him. They asked me if I would like to eat something, and judging by the not-too-appetizing appearance of the meal, I asked for some fresh fruit and/or vegetables. In addition to these things, they brought me leben and humus; my meal was satisfactory, to say the least!

Around midnight my husband was declared to be "under observation," and he was moved to a cubicle for the night. Since he couldn't sleep in the bed, and I was having difficulty sleeping on a chair, at about 3:30 a.m. he said he would sit in a chair, and I could have his bed. (That was a big kindness on his part!).

At 5:00 a.m. the nurses came along to say good morning. My husband was able to stop them from thinking I was the patient, or they would have hooked me up the various machines!

Throughout the day, whenever a meal was served to my husband, I was brought a meal as well. A man, who was visiting his mother, made the Sabbath morning *kiddush*, blessing on grape juice, for us. Along with each meal there were two rolls served so that we could make the special Sabbath blessing on bread.

My husband felt well enough to take the Sabbath elevator to the hospital synagogue for the afternoon prayer services, which we thought was at 1:20 p.m., but later discovered was at 7:00 p.m. Since we were already there at 1:00 p.m., we decided to wait to see if a prayer service would form. By 1:19 p.m. nine other men had miraculously appeared!

I discovered some copies of the *Torah Tidbits* newsletter in the synagogue. What a pleasure it was to read them, since I volunteer to fold them at the Israel Center every Thursday and love to read them every Sabbath.

It looks like God was really beaming His kindness on us and sending angels to help us. It was so apparent to us on that difficult day. Thank God for all those acts of kindness, and thank you for letting me have this vehicle in which to express it.

―᜵᜵᜵᜵᜵᜵᜵―

In Awe over Endless Kindness

I could write a book filled with the endless kindnesses we have received since the birth of our precious son. From the meals so generously provided during his hospitalizations, both to me while with him in the hospital, and to my not-small family; to the errands people do for us; to the volunteers who come—some to work with him and some to give some much needed and well deserved attention to his siblings; to the extra words of encouragement from neighbors when they see some small progress; to the effort that his "professional staff" (including several doctors, quite a few therapists, and the educational staff at his nursery) makes to make sure we know how much they care for him and appreciate him; to the volunteers who provide transportation—the kindness has just flowed unceasingly from the moment he was born.

I am in constant awe!

Stories Open My Eyes to the Abundant Kindness in the World

Today, while volunteering at Bikur Cholim Hospital in Jerusalem, I saw several lovely acts of kindness which really inspired me.

I was wheeling around a cart from the Hospital's gift shop with a young man, who has a slight physical handicap. We were selling mainly bottled water due to the high temperatures in Jerusalem for the last few days.

When we went to the X-ray department, two men were sitting and waiting for X-rays; one was in hospital pajamas, and the other was in regular clothing. The hospital patient said he would like a bottle of water, but when I informed him it was four NIS ($1), he said he had no money on him at the time. When I returned the bottle to the wagon (not realizing that I could have gotten him a cup of water from the sink), the man sitting next to him, a stranger, spoke up and said he would pay for the patient. What an amazing act of kindness from a stranger.

A few hours later, on another ward, I encountered two women patients confined to their beds in the same room. Both wanted large bottles of water, which we were out of on the cart. So I asked the young man volunteering with me if he would run down to the gift shop to get them bottles, which he graciously did. I was so pleased that we could cater to these two bed-bound ladies, since neither had guests visiting them at the time. I felt that the young man had really done a great act of kindness by his action.

On my way home from the hospital, a mentally disturbed man got on my bus. He told the bus driver that he had no money and insisted that as an "invalid" he should ride for free. He began arguing with the bus driver over this "free" ride. After a few stops, the driver told him to get off the bus, however the man had no intention of complying with him.

Having witnessed kind acts all day long, it occurred to me that I could pay for him. This would give the man his free ride and the driver a more peaceful drive.

The woman opposite me saw me reaching for my purse, and insisted on paying half, in order to do half of the *mitzvah*. I paid the driver, and gave the receipt to the handicapped man.

I am so grateful that God enabled me to do this act of kindness after having witnessing so many acts of kindness in the hospital.

I am also grateful for these daily email inspirations. They make me realize that there is abundant kindness in the world, and they open my eyes to see the good all around me.

May we all be blessed to see much kindness and to do acts of kindness whenever the situation arises.

Sick in Bed

I recently spent a week in bed sick with the flu. I was determined not to "feel sorry" for myself, and thought about what kindness I could do from my bed. Two opportunities presented themselves. The first was a phone call I received from a young woman who needed some advice about taking care of her new baby. I was happy to speak with her on the phone and answer her questions. The second was another phone call I received, this time from a neighbor, asking if her relatives could sleep at our house over the Sabbath. I was happy to be able to say "yes." Helping these two people definitely kept me in a happy mood when I was feeling so "down in the dumps," and who knows, maybe contributed to my getting well faster.

Understanding Pure Souls

Three years ago, after living in New York for eight years, we decided to move to Israel. Since we were expecting a baby, we agreed to wait until after the birth to move. When our sweet little boy was born the doctor kindly informed us that our newborn had Down syndrome! The world and our plans turned upside down!

A few months later life returned to normal (under the circumstances). After little Dovid had a tube inserted in his stomach and underwent open heart surgery, we continued with our plans. With much help and support from a wonderful organization called Nefesh B'Nefesh, we finally fulfilled our dream a year later and came home to Israel.

Once we settled somewhat, my wife Sara, who is a super special kindhearted woman, mentioned how there was a need for a support system for families with special children. In the U.S., our friends had given us a wonderful magazine called *Down's Syndrome Amongst Us*, written by a unique individual, Sara Sander, who herself has a child with Down syndrome; that magazine gave us much support and inspiration in those difficult early days.

My wife decided that she would publish a similar magazine in Hebrew. The only problem was that my wife did not know much Hebrew. Since she realized the importance of the feeling of support and encouragement, she decided it was something that must be done; she gathered articles and asked people to write personal stories; she even got the director of the National Center for Down Syndrome at Hadassah Hospital to write an article about all the medical issues.

A kind neighbor translated some items that were originally written in English. And, sure enough, just in time for Dovid's third birthday, the magazine was published. All the above was done while taking care of Dovid and our other children. She also gave birth nine months ago to a healthy baby girl.

When a neighbor mentioned that her sister just had a new baby with Down syndrome, we gave her a copy of the new magazine. She was able to read it and draw some emotional support and even smile, despite the situation. She was able to see that life has not ended; it has just taken a different twist. And as with many twists in life, we are often able to see how they do turn out for the best.

∾≈∾

A Special Woman
By C.K., Jerusalem

Although we had not planned it, my husband and I wound spending the Sabbath in a large Jerusalem hospital.

During the *Sabbath* services one woman was particularly hospitable to me. Although I didn't know her at all, she invited us to join her for a complete *Sabbath* dinner after the services and for meals the next day.

When my husband inquired if anyone knew of a place where I could sleep overnight, he was told to ask Mrs. Z. It turned out that Mrs. Z. was the woman who had been so helpful to me during the services. She was staying at the nearby motel and she invited me to stay with her for the night. What an act of kindness! I was truly blessed and may she be, too.

The next day we compared notes about our husbands who were patients on adjoining hospital wards. Then we wished each other's husband a speedy recovery and said goodbye.

A few hours later, when I returned to our parked car and turned the ignition on, I saw a warning light flashing on the dashboard. The person from the emergency roadside assistance service advised me that it would be unwise to drive the car until it was checked at the garage the next morning.

I was too tired to travel on the two buses that I needed to take to get home, so I called the office of the motel hoping to book a room, but there was no answer. As I turned back to the hospital building and mentally prepared myself to spend the night sitting in a chair by my husband's bedside, I almost tripped over my new friend, Mrs. Z. She was on her way back to the motel room for a third night. I explained my plight to her and she immediately invited me to spend another night at the motel with her. I was too shocked to refuse.

This "chance" meeting was assuredly another example of Divine providence, and again Mrs. Z., in her continuing kindness, was assuredly God's messenger!

∽꘧꘧꘧∾

Kindness Beyond Belief

An elderly friend of mine had to spend a week in a Jerusalem hospital. Although she had a daughter living nearby, it would have been very difficult for the daughter to spend so much time in the hospital, since her daughter had ten children at home and a full-time job that supported her family.

Another friend of mine, who is an older single woman and was a new friend to this woman, packed a suitcase with food and clothing and went to the hospital to stay with her for a few days to make sure her needs were attended to. No one asked her to go there, no one asked her to stay in the hospital. She just did it of her own accord. She slept in a chair by her friend's bed, and helped attend to her needs.

This kindness was such a great relief to the woman's daughter, who couldn't believe that someone would go so out of her way to extend such a major kindness. The family was very relieved and grateful to say the least.

Late Night Kindness

Our son with respiratory problems has been a catalyst for countless acts of kindnesses. It had been a few weeks since his last "rough spot" and we had thrown out the nose tube since it was... well... not so clean. (I will leave it to your imagination to figure out what a tube that had been in the nose of a two-year-old for over a week looked like.) We were counting on the two new ones we had received from the company that provides the oxygen, and hoping we would not need them.

Last week, at 11:30 at night, we noticed that his color was poor. We checked his saturation level and saw that he, indeed, needed oxygen. When we opened the new tube we found that it was far too small. My daughter found the phone number of an oxygen *gemach*, and at 11:45 at night a man drove across the city to bring us new tubes. He charged only the cost the *gemach* paid for the tubes, explaining apologetically that the *gemach* needs to keep a constant supply and therefore has to ask people to reimburse them for the cost of tubes, but not for the delivery across town at that late hour.

The Perfect Match

Mrs. Cohen volunteers at a hospital. The job she chose is caring for children in long term care, especially for children who are to some extent incapacitated. She talks with them, tells them stories, feeds them, washes them, and pampers them.

One day the food cart didn't show up on time. She waited, and waited, ten minutes... twenty minutes... no food cart.... An hour and still no food cart. "This is too much for these kids," she thought as she ran off to the office. She asked the secretary to call the manager of the kitchen to see what happened and to get the food up to the kids and fast.

While Mrs. Cohen was waiting with the secretary, the secretary asked her, "What about your forty-five-year-old bachelor son, hasn't he gotten married yet?"

"No he's still single. He's looking but has not found his match yet. We're on the border of despair already."

"Listen," said the secretary, "here's a phone number of a woman I know who seems to me to be a perfect match for your son, have him call her."

"He's not the type to call a woman he doesn't know."

"So you call her and start the conversation going. I feel sure it's worth it."

The couple got married last year and the volunteer who went out of her way to help severely ill children is due to be a happy grandmother in the next few days—all because of the act of kindness she did for severely ill children.

On The
Road

The Hitchhiker's Guide to Health

A nineteen-year-old student from my husband's *yeshiva* was hitchhiking in the Negev and accepted a ride from Sderot to Netivot from a stranger driving a new Volvo. The owner of the car was obviously rich.

The driver turned to the overweight and out-of-shape teenager and asked him, "Don't you care how you look? It's disgusting how overweight you are! You must take care of yourself!!"

The young man stammered that he tries but the food in the cafeteria is not the healthiest and he has no time for exercise.

The driver then said, "Go to the Dahan grocery store (next to the *yeshiva*) and tell them that I will pay 1,000 NIS ($250) a month for you to buy healthy food. I also expect you to exercise and to call me every month to let me know how you're doing."

The young student accepted the deal. He buys healthful foods, walks and watches snacks. After only two months, he already looks much better and is definitely heading in the right direction. He also doesn't even come near to spending 500 NIS ($125) a month at the grocery.

The concern of a stranger (and the monthly payments) did the trick.

A Prisoner of Kindness

While driving in Israel I generally slow down at bus stops and look to see if I can give anyone a lift.

One day I picked up a rabbi from a nearby *yeshiva* and gave him a lift to Jerusalem. He was grateful even though he had to squeeze into the back seat between the two car seats occupied by my granddaughters, Avigayil and Temimah.

After offering to take him home he told me I could drop him at the main bus stop instead of taking him all the way home to Bayit Vegan.

I thought to myself, "You know, he teaches at three different institutions. He must be tired."

I said, "Rabbi, you know, sitting between Avigayil and Temimah you're really my prisoner. I'm keeping you in custody until we reach Bayit Vegan!"

Needless to say he couldn't argue. After a long day he was really grateful.

Eight of Us in My Car

After my appointment in the city this morning, I picked up my daughter and the two of us continued home... or rather, the eight of us. It happened like this:

On the way to the highway, I spotted a youth looking for a

ride. When I told him where I was going, he asked if I could drop him off on the way. He shared his story about his high school experiences, and his hesitations about what to do after high school.

When I dropped him off, another young man appeared, also looking for a ride. He asked if I could let him off at the bus stop near Bnei Brak. He was on his way to the hospital in Beer Sheva where his sister was in serious condition after being hit by a car. Their parents were overseas. He had left Tzefat in a state of panic and shock as soon as he heard the news, misplacing his wallet and traveling by hitchhiking to reach his sister. I gave him some money, and he gave me his sister's name, so we could recite psalms for her recovery. When I left him off at the bus stop, there was another young man with a heavy knapsack trying to get to the next intersection. He got into the car, and on the way home we found three people from our community waiting at the intersection, looking for a ride home into the Shomron.

Sometimes I think these small kindnesses are more significant than some of the "more important" things that I accomplish during the day. I look for more opportunities to do these things because of the *Daily Dose of Kindness* emails, and it is with a sense of joy, knowing that there are so many people in the world doing similar acts of kindness. I wonder what the world would be like if these stories appeared on the front pages of our newspapers.

Strangers in the Night

About a month ago, my son, Yoram, was driving home to his village very late at night. When he found himself falling asleep at the wheel, he pulled over to the side of the road and fell asleep.

About 1:30 a.m. he woke up to the sound of knocking on the car window. He saw a woman and two small children standing there. The children were crying. The woman told him that she was in a taxi driving to Beer Sheva, when the driver received a call that he had to go to Tel Aviv, and he left her on the side of the road to hitchhike at night to Beer Sheva. She was stranded in the middle of nowhere, and didn't know what to do.

Yoram called his wife Sigalit and told her to prepare beds and food, because it was obvious that this family had not eaten for awhile.

He drove these perfect strangers to his home, and Sigalit first fed them "dinner" at 2 a.m. Afterwards, while she was bathing the dirty children, she discovered that they didn't even have underwear to wear. She gave them clothing, pajamas and underwear from her own children and dressed them. She then gave a package of clothing to the mother for the children.

In the morning, after breakfast, Yoram drove them to the central bus station in Jerusalem and gave them money for bus fare so they could go home, since the mother had no money on her.

A Lovely Act of Mutual Kindness

This morning as I was leaving my community for a meeting in Petach Tikvah, I stopped to pick up some young women who were hoping to find a ride to there. Their destination was close to mine.

This became a lovely act of mutual kindness, since I didn't know the way to the address to which I was headed, and my passengers did. With their directions, we all arrived where we wanted to be, on time.

The extra bonus was the feeling of happiness in my heart for the rest of the day after this experience of mutual kindness!

Kindness Is Contagious

I very much enjoyed Shmuel Greenbaum's talk in Ra'anana. It had a great impact on me, as you will see.

Last night, the city of Ra'anana organized a free Klezmer concert. On our way out of the amphitheater (away from the center of town, late at night) my wife overheard two women asking the security staff if there was any public transport in the area.

She approached the women and discovered that they needed to get back to Bnei Brak. We offered to take them into the center of Ra'anana, from where they hoped they could get a bus to the junction and then another bus to Bnei Brak.

Since we didn't know if there would still be buses to Bnei Brak, I phoned a taxi firm and asked them how much it would cost. When I heard how much the taxi wanted to charge, I decided to offer to take them all the way to Bnei Brak myself (after all, at that time of the night, it's only a fifteen-minute drive on empty roads). They were very grateful.

The down-side—they insisted on leaving me with money, despite us telling them that we don't do acts of kindness for cash!!

Would we have approached them without the memory of your talk? Perhaps. Perhaps not.

Hitchhiking in Faith

My friend and I were on our way to a Hassidic day of learning and meditation in the forests outside Jerusalem. We had tried to catch the bus but missed it, so we went down to a point on the outskirts of Jerusalem to hitch a ride.

"Maybe we should take a taxi," my friend said worriedly.

"Don't worry," I told her, "we'll get there. This is the right way to get to a Hassidic happening—through faith in God, miracles and the kindness of strangers!" I had no doubts whatsoever that one way or another, we would reach our destination.

Indeed, soon enough one car came along and dropped us down the road, another person picked us up at the next junction and took us very near the place. It seemed as if we would make it easily.

But then we somehow got lost and found ourselves walking in the heat down a never-ending gravel path. We stopped and I went to knock on the door of a random house in the adjoining community. A man answered and told us we had a six kilometer walk ahead of us. We looked at each other quite wearily and were thinking of what to do, when suddenly the man said, "I'll take you." He got his car keys and drove us there.

I was not surprised at all. My friend and I smiled all the way because it was so nice to feel God's blessing revealed in our lives and to see that this man was privileged, through his own kind impulses, to become God's instrument for this out-of-the-ordinary mode of travel. Actually the man seemed lonely and I imagine he was happy to be able to do something for someone else in such an unexpected way—so who knows how we touched his life?

When we got there we thanked him of course, since gratitude is an important part of this recipe for doing things on faith; and I could only bless him that he would have the opportunity to do many more kindnesses. I bless myself with the same thing—to belong to this lucky group of people who facilitate small miracles.

∽∰∽

Loving Memories

My daughter was going to a week-long seminar in Tel Aviv to prepare for a year of volunteer service. I took the hot rolls that I had prepared for her out of the oven and wrapped them in tinfoil, but with all the rush, she forgot to take them as she ran out of the house with my husband.

I called her on her cell phone to see if they were close enough to come back. It was too late—my husband had just dropped her off at the bus stop. Her bus was scheduled to arrive in fifteen minutes and it would take twenty minutes for my husband to pick up the rolls and bring them back to her.

So I grabbed the hot rolls and ran out to hitchhike to the bus stop in order to bring them to her in time. Of course she told me not to bother, but the following story which happened to me twenty-five years ago was on my mind and it inspired me to do this special favor for her:

A few minutes after my father and I had left home, on our way to New York, my mother, of blessed memory, noticed that I had left behind a favorite sweater that she knew I would want during my second year of university.

There were no cell phones in those days, so she jumped into the car, hoping she would catch up to us. But she had no reason to think that would really happen. About an hour-and-a-half after she left our home in Boston, she finally caught up to us at a rest stop in Connecticut that she and my father often used on their trips to New York. When we saw her, we thought we were hallucinating. But there she was, with my favorite sweater in hand.

With that story in mind I decided to go out of my way a bit to bring my daughter her hot rolls. The neighbor who gave me a ride to the bus stop was on his way to Jerusalem and offered to take my daughter to the place that she needed to go to catch her bus to Tel Aviv.

While she was on her way to Jerusalem, and I was hitchhiking back to my house, she sent me a beautiful text message on my cell phone thanking me for my efforts.

I'm sure she enjoyed those fresh, hot, whole wheat rolls.

His Kindness is Everlasting

As I was about to pull out of a Jerusalem parking lot, an elderly woman tapped on my car window. She asked if I could take her to a bus stop where a chartered bus would be coming to take her and others to a wedding. She was in quite a hurry to catch the bus on time. Although I was worried about losing my way through Jerusalem's one-way streets and arriving late for my next appointment, the opportunity to do this kindness spoke louder than my fear, so I agreed to get her to the bus stop on time.

She was so grateful that, as we drove together, she repeated over and over again in Hebrew, "Praise to God for His kindness is everlasting." She gave me a lesson about the security that Divine intervention gives us. It's always worthwhile to grab the opportunity to do a kindness, for God certainly sends us the right messengers to deliver the messages we are supposed to hear.

By the way, I did get to my appointment on time without getting lost. I suspect that this woman's deep love and faith in God had something to do with that.

The Straight Path in the Opposite Direction

I live in Maale Levona in Israel. I baby sit one-year-old twins a few mornings a week. The mother has to take one of the babies to therapists and doctors on a regular basis.

Since we are a small community, the buses do not run often and she is forced to sit and wait with the baby for long periods of time before a bus arrives. Yesterday she brought the baby by bus to a doctor in a nearby community. When she was finished, she faced a wait of several hours for the next bus. The doctor's receptionist went outside to see if anyone was going to another community in our area. A young man said he was.

He drove my friend to Shilo and asked where in Shilo she lived. When he found out she did not live there but in Maale Levona, he insisted on driving her home to Maale Levona. He would not even take a drink in thanks. He told her that he would not want his wife and baby sitting out in the hot sun waiting for a bus.

My friend found out later that he was actually on his way to Jerusalem, which is in the opposite direction. This act of kindness took him about an hour-and-a-half out of his way.

An Immediate Reward

A story about picking up a soldier hitching a ride to Jerusalem reminded me of a similar experience I had, in August 1987. I always made it a point to pickup soldiers on the road. As I turned off the Maale Adumim road into Jerusalem one Friday, I saw a soldier heading for the bus stop to Maale Adumim. Knowing that the bus did not run very often (Maale Adumim was a brand new town in those days), I turned around and went to offer him a ride to Maale Adumim. It turned out that the soldier was my own husband who had unexpectedly been given the weekend off! God certainly granted my desire to do a *mitzvah* with an immediate reward.

There Should Be More like Her

Ten years ago, I was making the two-hour drive to Jerusalem from Gush Katif with my infant son. It was a hot summer day and we did not have air conditioning, but I wanted to visit my sister-in-law who had just given birth to her first daughter. All of a sudden my car conked out on a main street at the entrance to Jerusalem. A woman stopped to help me find someone to help me get the car off the road.

Then, seeing how hot and tired I was, she bought me a drink and made sure that I fed my baby. She waited with me for about half an hour as I fed my baby. Then she lent me her cell phone to try to get help. (Cell phones were rare at that time in Israel.) When I was finally able to get the car started, she drove behind me from Givat Shaul to Bayit Vegan—(quite a long drive!) to make sure that I would not get stuck again.

I thanked her and asked who she was. She refused to tell me. I was able to find out from two women that were in her car at the time, a mother and daughter, that she was taking them to buy things for the daughter's upcoming wedding. Apparently they also needed her help. They told me that this woman is always busy doing kind deeds. I was amazed. I wanted to thank her for each thing she did, but she didn't stop until she was satisfied that my baby and I were 100% okay.

The People of Israel should have many more like her! It was a privilege for me to meet her. It was a very unusual experience.

⌐⌐⌐

Late Night Help

My son volunteers for the Magen David Adom (the Israel equivalent of the Red Cross) emergency medical service both in Jerusalem and in our community. One night he was called out to a car accident. Thank God no one was hurt, but the driver had two punctured tires. It was rather late on a Saturday night and the driver and his young children had to get back to a town quite far away. So one of the other volunteers drove home, brought his spare tire and helped change the two flat tires.

∽⊰⊱⊱∿

Wonderful Things Happen When You Do Little Things with No Expectation of Return

I was taking the bus from Jerusalem to Tzefat last year. At the scheduled rest stop, I noticed that a female soldier didn't buy anything. I know how little soldiers are paid, so I picked up a soft drink for myself and one for the female soldier. When I gave her the drink she asked why I bought it for her. I explained that I knew soldiers didn't make much money. She was grateful.

Most of the passengers got off at stops before the Tzefat bus station. I was the last person to leave the bus, with my suitcase-on-wheels which was very heavy. Since taxis do not stop at the bus station exit, I had to walk up a hill to a place where a cab would stop. As I struggled with pulling the suitcase up that very steep incline, the soldier that I had treated to a drink walked up to me and insisted on pulling my bag up the hill to a waiting taxi.

The taxi took me as far up the narrow steep street as he could go. When I started walking up the street, a young man came over and insisted on pulling my bag the rest of the way. Despite my offer to pay him, he would take nothing for his labor.

Wonderful things happen when you do little things without any expectation of return. I only gave a soldier a soft drink, but both she and a young man were able to do a *mitzvah* that I both needed and greatly appreciated.

No Ordinary Beggar

We were visiting Israel and getting confused in Jerusalem traffic jams during Ramadan. This was especially disconcerting because we were trying to get to the Har Nof home of a friend, Esther, in time for the Sabbath.

Wouldn't you know it, what we thought was a road, turned out to be an entrance to a parking lot! Here we were—stuck—as the precious moments ticked towards sunset. In front of us, a motorcycle on the sidewalk blocked the exit out of the parking lot. Beyond the parking lot was the busy road to Esther's, a can of "metallic and beeping worms." What could we do?

Along came an elderly beggar with a holy face. Dark soulful eyes, a long beard and the walk of a man on a mission characterized his arrival. I must admit we were nervous because he could represent a further delay and I was so worried we might accidentally desecrate the Sabbath. We nevertheless rolled down the window and my husband gave him some change. My husband didn't even look at the amount because our stress level was so high.

This was no ordinary beggar, however. The man glanced with interest at the coins, and motioned that he would help us. He moved the motorcycle blocking us from the road. Then he went into the middle of the street and stopped traffic to enable us to exit! We waved when we passed him as he conducted traffic and later arrived at Esther's just in time for the Sabbath.

The Messengers He Puts in Our Pathway

On the first day of the new school year, I was driving through the neighborhoods of Jerusalem to find the building where I was going to teach a course. Although I had given myself plenty of time to get there, or so I thought, I became hopelessly lost.

When I was already ten minutes late, I spotted two young men talking to each other by the side of the road. I stopped, rolled down my window, and asked them for directions. By this time, I was so anxious and frustrated while watching the time grow later and later, that even after they gave me directions, I was still not sure about how to get to my destination.

One of them then offered to take me to my destination. He got into my car, and within five minutes, directed me to the doorway of the building where I was teaching. I don't know how he returned to his friend, but I was grateful for his wholehearted kindness.

Thank God for these messengers that He puts in our pathway to guide us!

Gratitude Makes Us Happy

When I think of kindness stories, I try to think of the BIG major ones. The little ones sometimes go unnoticed. It's nice to notice them, because they are all around us.

Today was one of those days. I felt as if there were angels, right here on earth, making sure my day went smoothly. I drove to Jerusalem, planning to park as soon as I entered the city because I was anxious about driving on crowded, busy streets. I thought I could take a taxi to an important meeting, but since I had no money in my purse, I decided to drive into the city.

I called a friend to guide me to the address. Since there was a general strike in the country, she was home and guided me by phone to my destination.

Parking was the next challenge. Finding parking in the middle of the day in Jerusalem is next to impossible. When I got to the address, there was a huge parking space right in front of the building. After I parked, a kind gentleman appeared from nowhere at my window to tell me I was too far from the curb and he would help guide me back into the space. After I re-parked, the gentleman disappeared even before I could thank him.

As I was wondering if I had any coins in my wallet to put into the parking meter, a lovely woman approached me and mentioned that since there is a strike, there is no need to put money in the parking meters.

I hoped that my meeting would go as kindly as the morning had. Sure enough, the two hour meeting passed quickly and pleasantly.

As I prepared to drive home, I looked up and said a big "THANK YOU!" The day is filled with more happiness when we notice the small kindnesses around us and remember to say "thank you!"

I'll Take You to School

Since I have been reading these emails, not only have I been motivated to do more acts of kindness, but I have also been on the lookout to see all of the acts of kindness that others are constantly doing for me.

On the bus I took to work this morning, there were two small children going to school. Before they noticed, they missed their stop. They called out to the driver, who answered them: "Don't worry, I'll take you to school," and he did! Right to the door!

Everybody on the bus was very impressed and happy with the driver's kind deed.

Come with Me

Many years ago, a friend and I were trying to go somewhere in Haifa. We had no idea how to get there and neither of us spoke Hebrew well. We told a bus driver where we needed to go. He said "come with me." After he finished his route, he drove us right to the door.

～※✦※～

Right to Their Door

In the early 1980's, during a sabbatical year in Israel, we took our young children on a bus journey from Jerusalem to Hadera, where we were to spend a couple of days visiting my husband's relatives. They had given us directions via bus to their home.

It was a good long trip by bus between the two cities and, once in Hadera, we waited with our kids and suitcases at Hadera's little central bus station until the local bus arrived. As we rode along the semi-rural bus route, my husband gave the bus driver the street name of our destination. We were quite alarmed to learn that the bus driver was not familiar with the street we named (this was before cell phones and we had no means of contacting our relatives to get further directions).

While we sat there trying to decide what to do the bus driver suddenly asked, "What is the name of the family?"

My husband replied, "Abarbanel."

"Abarbanel?!" yelled the bus driver, "Why didn't you say so before?" And then he proceeded to drive us right to the door of our relative's home.

The Bus Driver who Taught Love

A friend told me that whenever her daughter goes onto a bus in Jerusalem, someone always helps her with her baby and stroller and gives her a seat.

A few weeks ago she got onto a bus and no one helped her. The bus driver announced to the passengers: "This bus is not moving until someone helps this lady and gives her a seat."

How easy it is to think only about our own needs and forget the needs of others. How fortunate are we for those who remind us.

I know you are wondering. Yes... several people ran to help her. The bus took off right away. And the bus driver acquired the title of *"Rebbe"* when he taught a bus load of passengers what it means to "Love your neighbor as you love yourself."

Planting Smiles in the Streets of Jerusalem

While I was studying in Jerusalem, I was waiting for the bus to the university one day on King George Street. A modestly dressed middle-aged Israeli man standing next to me offered me a red carnation.

Soon, I noticed he offered one to another woman who came to the bus stop. Every time a bus approached the stop, he went in to give one to the driver. When he ran out of flowers, he simply got on the bus and left.

It amazed me that he was doing this out of his own kindness, and I'm sure, reminded everyone how light can shine even in the midst of hard times.

Caring for Injured Passengers

My aunt was looking for a seat on an Egged (an Israeli bus company) bus when she fell down. She cried out in pain. Her fellow passengers tried to help her and make her comfortable while the bus driver pulled the bus to the side of the road and called the Egged office. The driver told headquarters to send another bus since he was leaving off all the passengers. He then proceeded to drive my aunt straight to the nearest first-aid station and made sure she received immediate help. [She had broken vertebrae in her spine that have subsequently healed.]

This is obviously Egged's official policy if someone is injured. When anyone hears this story they exclaim "Only in Israel!"

Kindness Is As Kindness Does
By C.K., Jerusalem

It was the first time I had taken an Egged bus from Bnei Brak to Jerusalem. Before I boarded, I had asked the driver if he drove "to Jerusalem." "Yes, Ma'am," he replied. However, I neglected to ask where in Jerusalem.

As it turned out, the bus did indeed go "to Jerusalem" but it did not go to the Central Bus Station where my car was parked. After each local stop in Jerusalem I was expecting the bus to turn around and proceed to the Central Bus Station. No such luck.

At twenty minutes after midnight I still sat in the now-empty bus. The driver asked me why I wasn't getting off. I said I was "waiting for the Central Bus Station stop." In my broken Hebrew and his broken English the driver asked if anyone waiting at that bus shelter could explain to me in English that this was the last stop for that evening. I finally understood that I would have to take a taxi from there to the Central Bus Station since no buses were running at that hour of the night.

As it turned out, God and the driver had compassion on me—the driver allowed me to remain on the bus as he was returning to park at the Central Bus Station for the night.

As I quickly walked toward my car parked on the deserted street near the Central Bus Station, I saw an older woman also walking quickly in the same direction. I decided that I would offer her a ride to wherever she needed to go. After all, hadn't the bus driver done me a great kindness? But first I called my husband to tell him that I was on the way to the car.

By the time I had actually started the car I had forgotten my resolve to offer the woman a ride to her home. However, in His kindness, God did not allow me to forget my resolve. The lady quickly came running up to my car and asked for a ride, asking whether I was going to "such and such street."

In truth, I had never heard of "such and such street." But my standard answer when offering someone a ride is always "Yes!" After all, searching for "such and such street" by car, even if it is in completely the opposite direction from where I am planning to go, is never so hard as walking there by foot when it is late at night and one may not have the money to pay for a taxi.

I was glad that the lady had come up to ask me and I was happy to oblige her request. After letting her off at her street I proceeded to make a few wrong turns as I tried to find my way back home from this unfamiliar area of Jerusalem. But God helped me again. Before very long I was back again on familiar roads.

I was pleased to have been able to return the bus driver's kindness so soon by being allowed to do an act of kindness for another person. As the saying goes, "Kindness is as kindness does."

Mysterious Helpers
By C.K., Jerusalem

I was driving down a busy, narrow street in an old Jerusalem neighborhood. I edged to the right to make way for an oncoming police car. However, I edged too far and I ended up wedged under the bumper of a parked car.

I was invited to vacate my car by a passerby who offered to maneuver the car for me. Then, quicker than I could comprehend what was happening, five black-clad religious men, also passing by, grabbed onto my car and in one graceful and coordinated lift disengaged my car from the bumper of the parked car. Then my unsung helpers disappeared as quickly as they had appeared.

This was truly kindness to me and kindness to my car. May God bless them!

He Thanked ME
By Shulamit Wolfe Stander

One evening I took a one-mile walk to a supermarket in the next neighborhood. I knew I needed to pick up a couple of things, and I figured that my "evening walk" was a good time to get two things done. As often happens, two things turned into three bags full of groceries and household items.

I started the walk home, and encountered many vehicles parked mostly on the sidewalk, forcing me to walk in the street with the laden bags. A few cabs slowed down as they passed, gesturing to check if I wanted a ride. I didn't have any cash on me, and knew that I could usually handle the walk home, so I nudged them on.

After a short time, my asthma was starting to get the best of me, due to carrying too much, as well as the long walk home. One young cab driver pulled over from his lane, almost forcing me to stop, as he wedged me between his car and the parked vehicles. He offered to drive me home, but I again refused. I told him that I didn't have cash, and that I was halfway home already.

He insisted that I get in, since it was dangerous for me to be walking in the road (though he saw I had no choice!), and that I shouldn't worry about the fare. He said if his aunt or mother were in the same situation, he'd like to think someone would do the act of kindness and pick them up, as well.

He didn't even know how much I really did need the help, as my asthma was really acting up. He let me off in my neighborhood, by a wide sidewalk, at the top of an easy, downhill walk to my house, and wished me well. I thanked him profusely. He thanked ME for the opportunity to help out. What a *mentsch* (good fellow).

I Love Taxi Drivers in Israel

In 1979 I was in Israel for my second year of seminary. I had stayed with a friend of mine at a mutual acquaintance's apartment in Netanya for the Sabbath. On Sunday morning we needed to return to Jerusalem to attend classes at the seminary. We always traveled either via public buses or we hitchhiked. For some reason, neither of us had remembered to bring money with us for the trip back, so we resorted to hitchhiking.

We went to the intersection, where everyone would go to hitchhike. But for some reason we were unable to secure a ride. We tried for nearly two hours with no luck. This had NEVER happened to us.

Finally, we walked over to a garage where there were taxis and attempted to get a ride home. We explained our predicament and told the driver that we would pay him when we arrived in Jerusalem. The driver asked us a few questions about ourselves—were we religious, where we came from, etc. He then agreed to take us and we proceeded on our way in his taxi.

He was a nice man and we found ourselves thoroughly enjoying conversing with him. When we arrived at the school, we both went into the dorms to get our money and pay him. When we came out he was gone. The security guard told us that the taxi driver told him to tell us that the ride was on him and that he so enjoyed his conversation with us, that it would suffice as payment for the ride!

Needless to say, we were stunned! I love taxi drivers in Israel. I have had several great experiences with them.

∽✲✲✲∽

The Soldier, the Cab Driver
and the Expectant Mother

On the morning before Passover, when I was six months pregnant, I took the bus into Jerusalem. My in-laws lived a few short blocks away from the Central Bus Station in Kiryat Moshe, and normally I walked. Unfortunately, buses did not mix well with my pregnancy, and by the time I got off the bus I was violently ill.

It was quite close to the time of day when the buses were going to stop running, but a young soldier on his way to Haifa insisted on taking me in a cab to my in-laws. I was very worried about his making the last bus to Haifa, but he insisted he would be fine.

He was, because the cab driver, who not only refused to take money for taking us to Kiryat Moshe, also assured me that he would bring the soldier right back to the bus station so he would not miss his bus.

∼⁓⁓

When We Are Pleasant to One Another, the Ride through Life is More Pleasant

We've all heard stories about taxi drivers who "took their passengers for a ride," but one day I had the pleasure of riding with a Jerusalem cab driver who was kindness personified.

That morning I had bought a new chair for my home office—the bulky kind on wheels—and since I don't have a car, I had to hail a cab to take the chair home. Naturally it was a rainy morning and of course I live in a northern neighborhood of Jerusalem, which some cab drivers don't want to go to because it is so far out; and of course, I needed to find a cab driver willing to put the chair in the back seat of his taxi.

I waited a few minutes and there wasn't a cab in sight. I was about to call a taxi company to order a cab when a taxi pulled up beside me. The driver cheerfully put my chair in the back seat and said it was no problem at all to go to my neighborhood. During the half-hour drive we discovered we have many things in common: we both have a great love of the Land of Israel; we both have apartments with magnificent views of the desert; he drives handicapped children to and from their special kindergarten every day and I occasionally do public relations work for organizations that help these children, and on and on.

When we got to my apartment building, which is down one flight of stairs from street level, the taxi driver asked me if I could manage with the chair on my own. I said I could since I figured the taxi ride was going to be expensive enough as it was, without paying extra for the "delivery service" down the stairs. But apparently the driver was not convinced by my answer because before I could even get out of the car, the driver told me to watch the taxi while he carried the chair down the stairs.

When I asked him how much the fare came to, not only did he not ask for a "tip" for carrying the chair, but he didn't even charge me extra for transporting the chair—which he was entitled to do. And to top off everything, the price he charged me was about 20% less than what taxi drivers usually charge for the journey.

This is not the first time that I have been shown kindness by a Jerusalem taxi driver, and I think what makes the difference (sometimes) between good and bad service is the "service" we give to others.

When we are pleasant to one another, the ride through life is more pleasant, too.

⚬⟞⟝⟞⟝⟞⟝⟞⟝⚬

We Have to Stick Together and Help Each Other Out

Once I was in a cab with a driver who had lost a leg in one of the wars. I happened to be on the way to the municipality to arrange for a discount in our property taxes to which we were entitled because of our handicapped child. This came out in conversation during the ride, at which point he switched off the meter, saying "we have to stick together and help each other out." He also offered to take me home after I was finished.

Maybe Someday I Could Help Him Too

I was rescued by an Israeli taxi driver. I had been on a hike with a friend. When my friend's car broke down on our drive back home, I used my cell phone to call a taxi driver who I had previously used several times.

Although I had no cash on me, I thought that he might let me get money from my apartment to pay him after we arrived home. Sure enough, he came immediately to pick me up, but he refused to let me pay him when I arrived back home.

Instead, he told me that he was glad to be able to help me and maybe someday I could help him too.

Emotional First Aid

As registered nurses, it was natural that my co-worker and I stopped to help at a car accident on our way home.

Two solo drivers were involved. One was a young Jewish woman from a nearby town. The other was an Arab man from the Arab village just down the road. Both of them were very close to their homes and obviously on their way home when the accident occurred.

My co-worker, tended to the young woman, who, as it turned out, was someone she knew. The young woman was not injured badly, but was pretty shaken up and sitting on the road crying.

I tended to the Arab man who was in worse condition, lying near his car in obvious pain. After examining him, I saw there was not much for me to do for him other than make him comfortable, and wait for the ambulance.

I made sure that someone who spoke Arabic contacted his family, and gathered his personal belongings that were scattered around him on the road. I placed his eyeglasses carefully into his shirt pocket, and his cell phone deep in his pants pocket.

The ambulance came and loaded both of them, the man on a stretcher and the young woman sitting beside him. Her mother had arrived in the meantime and was in the ambulance talking with the daughter.

The police had just arrived when the son of the wounded man appeared. Obviously very shook up, he tried desperately to get to his father, inside the ambulance. The police officer pulled him back and told him to keep his distance. This agitated the upset son even more, and soon there was shouting and shoving going on.

This is where I stepped in. It was obvious to me that this was a person who was very upset and worried about his father and was getting no information or assistance in finding out that his father was okay.

I led him out of reach of the agitated police and explained to him that I am a nurse and that I had attended his father after the accident. I asked if he wanted to know details. He immediately calmed down and listened to my explanations, including where I placed his father's eyeglasses and cell phone.

I then made sure that he was allowed to see his father in the ambulance and to be reassured that he was not seriously injured. I made sure that he was driven by a friend to meet his father at the hospital, explaining to the friend that the son was too upset to drive, and that he needed to be accompanied to the E.R.

I feel that I acted as anyone in my profession should. I felt personally satisfied that I was able to help in a way that went beyond physical fist aid, by giving emotional first aid to a worried son.

The Trucker From Heaven

A few days ago, I was driving on the busy highway from Efrat to Jerusalem, when suddenly I felt like I had a flat tire. I got out of my car, put on my yellow jacket and went to confirm my suspicion.... I was correct. So I stood by my car trying to figure out what to do.

Suddenly from the other side of the busy highway a man in a truck stopped, honked his horn and backed up. He got out of his truck, crossed over to my side of the highway and I showed him my flat tire. He went into my trunk and tried to get out my spare tire but it was stuck in there very tightly and would not come out. To make matters worse, it was flat. He took off the flat tire from my car and told me he would be back in half an hour with another tire and he drove off.

A police jeep came by and saw my tire. The officer asked if I needed help. I told him I was being helped so he told me he was going to send a jeep of soldiers to watch me.

In a few minutes a jeep of soldiers came and the man came

back with a tire and put it on. One of the soldiers was talking with the truck driver and found out that he was a Bedouin Arab from Beersheva.

Since one of the soldiers spoke English I told him to tell the truck driver in Hebrew that he is an angel from heaven and ask him what do I owe him. The truck driver told the soldier that I don't owe him anything and he drove off.

It is so very frightening for me when these situations occur because of I have a communication disability which forces me to write things out in order to communicate... but there is always God watching over me and taking very, very good care of me.

Thank you God and thank you mankind.

Family Life at Holiday Time

✑

My Son the "Angel"

One of the members of our community was diagnosed with cancer. As soon as he told me, I made him a nice homemade *challah* (bread) for the Sabbath. The next time I saw him, he told me how delicious it was and that he hopes that God will cure him, but if anything will help him in his recovery; it will be that delicious *challah*.

I told my daughter how good he made me feel by saying that, and she asked me if I made him another *challah* the following week. I hadn't thought to do that, but she said that if he is saying the *challah* will help him, I must make one for him every week!

I realized that she was correct, and so I've been sending one every week with my six-year-old son. (It is his act of kindness and not mine that is the reason why I am writing this story.) He delivers the *challah* every week, rain or shine—sometimes it has really been raining hard.

We live in a closed community in Gush Etzion so it isn't dangerous or very far for him to go on his own, but for a young child it is still an effort. However, he happily does it every week as soon as he comes home from school, because he knows the man is ill and that it is a big *mitzvah*.

He came home very excited one week and said that the man's wife called him her "angel." Recently they started giving him a little candy bar whenever he delivers the *challah*, but he was happily delivering it even before he got the physical thank you from them.

This week, it was getting very late and my son wasn't home

yet from school and I had to drive my daughter to catch a bus, so we figured we should drop off the *challah* on the way. When she brought the *challah* to the door, the wife asked where my son was!

I think that my son's delivery of the *challah* has become even more special to the man (and his wife) than my making it.

Truly Inspiring

My daughter is in her senior year of high school. In Israel there is a program called *shelef* which is the Hebrew acronym for *shminiyot leayara pituach* (seniors to development towns). Participants leave home and move into a poor development town to try to raise the level of the children in the school. My daughter is living in a housing project with three other girls.

Last weekend she and one of her roommates, who are also from our community, invited the entire class to our community for the Sabbath. She wrote to the mayor of our town to get help and he funded a bullet-proof bus to bring the girls back and forth (we live in Gush Etzion).

The girls ate at the homes of families in our community on Friday night, and then came to an *oneg* (celebration) at our house. On the Sabbath morning they had a communal lunch. On Saturday night, right after the Sabbath ended, we had a *melave malka*, the traditional festive meal celebrated at the departure of the Sabbath.

Since my father always tells me to spend any money I want on special charity projects, and he'll be only too happy to reimburse me, I made a *melave malka* pizza party in my house on Saturday night. I knew it would be a nice way to end the weekend for these girls. My daughter also invited over her friends from her old school and they brought musical instruments and made a really beautiful *melave malka* for these girls.

The girls could not stop talking about the wonderful weekend. Some of these girls didn't even own a skirt and had to run out on Friday to buy one for the Sabbath. They said they had never seen such a beautiful Sabbath, and they want to have homes just like they saw here in our community. They said the respect that they saw all family members give each other was truly inspiring and they even asked my daughter to find them religious boyfriends (which is a good sign of their interest!). Suddenly my daughter and her friends from the program are the most popular girls in town. The entire high school was talking about the weekend in our community, and the girls who didn't come for whatever reason are so disappointed that they missed out and are looking forward to the next time we have such a weekend.

Previously, it had been hard for my daughter and her friends from the program to connect to these girls. They come from very, very different backgrounds and cultures and have different priorities. But the ice has been broken and they now feel they can truly accomplish what they set out to do. The weekend involved a lot of work and planning—they had to beg the girls to come and I received numerous phone calls from my daughter, worried that no one would show up. However, getting such wonderful feedback made it all worthwhile.

Candles of Light

My father was Rabbi Nachman Bulman. He taught *Torah* in Jerusalem for the last twenty-five years of his life, and counseled thousands of people from all walks of life.

Yesterday, when I lit my father's *yahrzeit* (memorial) candle at the onset of the Sabbath, a story came to mind that he once told me. It was a small incident, but worth remembering.

About twelve years ago, when my father was the spiritual leader of a community in Migdal Ha'emek, he underwent surgery in nearby Haifa. There were complications. My father was very ill; he drifted in and out of consciousness for two or three days. My mother, or one of my brothers, stayed with him almost constantly, but late on Friday afternoon, my mother went home to make the Sabbath and my father found himself alone. As far as anyone knew, he was unconscious, but in fact, he was partly awake at times.

He knew that it was close to the Sabbath, and he was very, very depressed. He was thinking that he was all alone in the hospital and that there would be no Sabbath for him—nothing to make this day any different from any other day in the ICU. While he was immersed in black and gloomy thoughts, two nurses came into his room.

One of them said, in Hebrew, "I am going to light candles in here."

The other one said, "What for? The patient is unconscious, anyway."

The first nurse said, "Even if he is, he is a big rabbi and spiritual leader and would want Sabbath candles in his room."

Although his eyes were still closed, my father heard her light the candles and say the blessing. She said *"Shabbat Shalom"* and left the room. At that moment his spirits were enormously lifted, and the oppressive gloom was gone.

My father recounted this story as an example of how a seemingly small act of kindness can help someone in a very big way. It was also, for him, an example of the kind of thing that distinguishes life in Israel. That nurse was not religious, though she was perhaps traditional, but she had respect for a rabbi and sensitivity to what he needed, beyond his immediate medical needs.

My father was tremendously grateful to her. He could not pray or make the *kiddush* blessing on the wine on the Sabbath or do anything for himself. Without that nurse's thoughtful gesture, he would have had no Sabbath at all.

❦

Help with a New Baby

My neighbor went to England with her family at the end of June to have her baby near her parents, and to be with them for the Jewish holidays. They are returning home Thursday, at midnight. I wanted to invite them for a meal for their first Sabbath back in Israel, but we will not be home. So I cooked them chicken with vegetables, rice and *kugel* (baked pudding) and put it in their refrigerator for them to enjoy on their first Sabbath home since their baby was born.

The bigger act of kindness though was really on her part.

Last year when I was the one with a new baby, she walked my child to kindergarten every single day, and brought her home too, just so I would not have to go out with my newborn. I offered to pay her, but she would not accept money to do an act of kindness.

Giving Up Her Seat

My five year-old daughter is such a good girl and tries so hard to do nice things that I promised her I would write this story about the act of kindness she did, so others can learn from her.

Every Sabbath our five-year-old daughter sits next to me at the dining room table while our three-year-old daughter sits opposite me.

For some reason, our three-year-old took it into her head last Sabbath that she wanted to sit where her older sister usually does, and she would not let up on it.

My husband and I tried to dissuade her. But it was no use. She continued to moan and *kvetch* (complain) about it and hang around by my elbows disconsolately.

Suddenly, her older sister picked herself up and moved across the table to her younger sister's seat. The look of joy on our three-year-old's face was something to see. We are so proud of the really big act of kindness our oldest daughter did for her little sister, by willingly giving up her usual seat for no reason other than that her little sister wanted it so badly. And she did it the next day at lunch as well!

A Grand Grandson

I recently had hand surgery. My husband and I spent the first Sabbath after the surgery with our daughter and her family in Jerusalem. We stayed in an apartment about a block away from their apartment. I was quite handicapped after the surgery, especially since it was done to my right hand and I am right-handed.

When it was time to return to our apartment after lunch, for a Sabbath rest, I wanted to bring a book there but dreaded the thought of carrying it, since it was difficult for me. As I stood there debating with myself about whether I should take the book, my six-year-old grandson, Zevy, showed me his bag and said that he had a pretty big bag and that it was big enough to hold my book. He said that I should put the book in his bag and that he would carry it for me. I was so thrilled that Zevy had offered to do this without anyone asking him. He carried the book for me and we both were very happy.

My Happiest Birthday

I work in a school in Jerusalem for boys who come from England and America to study post high school. I have been working there for five-and-a-half years now. I consider it a great honor that I am able to be involved in these boys' lives.

I cannot tell you how wonderful and special each boy is to me. Many of them are far away from home for the first time in their lives. They miss their families and their families miss them.

Our school is small; about forty boys study here. Thus one is able to get to know the boys and their individual needs. It is also possible to watch each one grow as they learn about life and themselves through the study of *Torah*.

I make meals for the boys daily as well as for the Sabbath and holidays. Every day, without fail, each boy thanks me for the meal and most of them offer to help out. The boys like to make salad, bake, peel vegetables and even help make *kreplach* (dumplings). You name it and they are usually more than happy to help out. I feel it is good for them as well as me, so when they have a break in their studies, I let them help out.

Three years ago, two wonderful boys were responsible for serving the evening meals as well as those on the Sabbath and Yom Tov (holidays). They did their best to serve the meals nicely, which is important to me since I work hard to prepare them.

One of these boys had discovered when my birthday was, and when it came close to the date, collected money from all of the other boys to make a surprise for me. When I arrived at work on the morning of my birthday, I opened the kitchen door and received a shock!

The entire kitchen was decorated with streamers hanging from the ceiling and strung every which way; balloons were stuck in the ovens and in pots and every spot imaginable. There were "*Mazal Tov!*" ("Good Luck!") signs on the ceiling and walls and "Happy Birthday" balloons on the refrigerator as well as a card and a "Happy Birthday" banner signed by everyone. They wrote the cutest things.

They gave me a newly released book and a spoon spatula on which they had engraved "Our headmistress" on it. Such sweetness.

In all of my life nobody has ever done such an amazing and wonderful thing for me, especially on my birthday!

∽⦃⦃⦄∽

With the Love and Support of His Friends

A terrible accident occurred recently in our community in which a teenage boy was badly burned. He was rushed to the hospital where he received prolonged treatment.

His youth group leaders immediately rallied support from this boy's friends. They arranged shifts for all the boys to visit their friend in the hospital, so that he would be surrounded by friends at all times. This meant they had to take off from school and travel long distances.

Even on the Sabbath they arranged places for the boys to stay, so their friend would be surrounded by his friends on the Sabbath.

With God's help, and with the love and support of his friends, this boy recovered.

Remembering the Hungry During Celebrations

While we were busy planning a wedding for our son and future daughter-in-law, we were delighted to find out that many people use this time of celebration to help others. For example, after every wedding at the catering hall we selected, the leftover food is donated to the needy through two charities, Ezer Mizion and Yad Sarah.

On the Sabbath before the wedding we made a celebratory *kiddush* where many foods were served. After the Sabbath, Table to Table, another organization that collects food for the needy came with refrigerated trucks to collect the food that was not eaten.

Another beautiful custom that is observed in honor of the marriage of a new couple is that the families donate money to an organization to prepare a special dinner on the night of the wedding for those in need.

The Lone Soldier

My husband teaches at the Har Etzion *Yeshiva* in Gush Etzion. He and all the other teachers frequently invite students to their homes for the Sabbath meals. One of his students, an American whose parents live in the U.S., spent the last nine months in the Israeli army. Whenever he was notified at the last minute that he was getting off for the Sabbath from the army, he would call us and ask if he could join us for Sabbath meals. It was always a pleasure to have him.

During one of the meals he had with us, we somehow got to talking about a beautiful Lenox vase that we had received for a wedding present, which a guest had once accidentally broken. Our post-army *yeshiva* guest returned to Israel a few days ago, after a two week visit to his parents in the U.S. After the Sabbath he showed up with a gift. I took one look at the shape of the box and realized right away what it was—a beautiful Lenox vase with gold trim. I thanked him profusely for his kindness and told him it was not necessary.

But even more beautiful than the vase, was the note he put in the box. He thanked us for our warmth and told us how much he felt at home with us. He explained that all the meals he enjoyed with us on the Sabbath helped to make the experience of being a *chayal boded* (lone soldier - a soldier whose family is not in the country), all that much easier.

I am grateful to this young man for teaching me how important our warmth and hospitality is to our guests. I had never realized it before.

─❦─

Anywhere in Israel

As an American seminary student studying in Israel, it often becomes very hard and overwhelming to make plans to go away for the Sabbath every week. Especially for girls who have no family in Israel or for other girls who want to visit incredible families but just end up going to the same family friends every week, making Sabbath plans just becomes very stressful.

The one thing that makes the whole experience easier and more meaningful is the act of kindness done by one family. They run a service known as "Anywhere in Israel" which you can call up and ask to be placed for the Sabbath with a nice family anywhere in Israel.

Within a couple of days of "putting in your order," they get back to you with your sleeping arrangements and all your meals set. They do it with such joy and enthusiasm and tell you how great each family is before you go. It's really an incredible thing that they do and such a tremendous act of kindness for me and the other hundreds of seminary students here for the year.

I'm Thinking of You and I Care

I enjoy the *Daily Dose of Kindness* emails. It's nice to know that there are people out there doing a little each day, just because they can.

I bake *challah* every week for the Sabbath. Each week I take one or two *challahs* to a different person in my neighborhood. I give the *challah* to people who have been sick, feeling down, a bit lonely or have a *simcha* (festive family celebration), coming up.

The message I try to give people through my *challah* is: "I'm thinking of you and I care."

Challah Classes

I hire a Russian lady to help me with doing laundry, ironing, babysitting, and other household chores for two or three hours a week. Thank God, she has become a sort of *bubby* (grandma) for us and she really looks forward to her time in our house, and with our kids.

I bake a tremendous amount—every kind of delicacy. I especially enjoy perfecting Sabbath *challahs*. In truth, I have recently started teaching these things for pay.

My Russian helper has asked me repeatedly to teach her how to make *challahs*, but so far it has never worked out, since making *challahs* really takes an entire day. Sometimes I have to split up the job, and make the dough the night before, and shape and bake the next day. Otherwise, between all my other obligations, I don't finish it in one day.

I finally decided that I should make the time for her. Although it was difficult for me, I split up the tasks to fit her schedule.

For several weeks in a row she shaped the loaves with me. One day, I made the dough with her in the morning, even though it meant that I was literally shaping and baking until very late at night and had to do the dough in two stages, since the kids came home for lunch in the middle. It was so rewarding. We BOTH had a great time.

⌐~✶✶✶~⌐

A Cake for the Kids

I heard that my neighbor gave birth to a baby girl. I met her husband in the supermarket that Friday morning with three kids, shortly before she was released from the hospital.

I knew other neighbors were cooking meals, but I decided to send over a chocolate cake. She called me after the Sabbath to say I had made her kids' Sabbath, since she obviously did not have the time to bake.

⌐~✶✶✶~⌐

Birthday Messengers
By Shulamit Wolfe Stander

Today was my son's eighteenth birthday. He was spending it in his *yeshiva* in Neve Yaakov, where he dorms all week, since they are having a *yeshiva* Sabbath (a Sabbath when all the boys remain in the *yeshiva*).

Although he didn't want us to make any fuss over him, even till he's 120, he'll still be my baby, so I really wanted to send something to him for his birthday. Remembering something I picked up for him during the week, that he could use in *yeshiva*, I posted a message to the local Har Nof neighborhood email list, and one to the Neve Yaakov email list, on the off chance that someone from there was in Har Nof this morning, and would be going back before the Sabbath.

I got my first call minutes after I posted the message, from an acquaintance who passed by a young man in her lobby, talking on a cell phone, who she overheard saying that he would soon be on his way back to Neve Yaakov. When she walked into her house and saw the email from me, she ran down to catch him. He agreed to take the package and my husband ran over with it.

He not only was going to the neighborhood, but was willing to find my son's *yeshiva* building and make sure it got to him, hand delivered.

I got a few more phone and email offers, and as if that wasn't incredible enough, I received the following email:

"Dear Mother of Neve Yaakov student, I am in Neve Yaakov. If you don't find a messenger, maybe I can send over a little gift package 'from' you. What type of thing would you like to send him? I have odds and ends in the house which might make nice presents including a huge amount of NEW Tupperware. Let me know if you are stuck."

I am always amazed at the incredible workings of God, and delighted by the phenomenal capacity for kindness which He instilled in His people.

The One Who Does Kindness for Us All the Time

One night I got home late from work. I was exhausted. But when my wife told me that a newly married couple needed a few more people to join them for their *sheva brachos* celebration, I was delighted to help with this great *mitzvah*. My son had already agreed to go, so the two of us ran out to catch a bus to the festivities.

The kindness that we did for the young couple was repaid last Friday when my wife needed medical treatment an hour before the Sabbath. We were able to get a taxi right away to take us to the doctor's office, which was located a few miles from our home. But by the time we finished, it was half-an-hour before candle lighting time and there weren't any taxis or buses available on the streets of Jerusalem so close to the Sabbath. So my wife and I started walking home. There were no cars on the road and if we walked the entire way, my wife would not make it home in time to light candles.

After walking for five minutes, a car drove by and suddenly stopped next to us as the driver motioned for us to get in—it was the bride and groom whose *sheva brachos* my son and I had just attended. They were going to their parent's house and drove us right to our doorstep. Miraculously, we had made it home in time for candle lighting.

~※※※~

Three Angels
By Chava Dumas

Nearly seven years ago I gave birth to twins on the Sabbath. The following Friday night, we were hosting in our home the traditional *shalom zachor* celebration for our son. After synagogue the following morning, we would be making his *bris* as well as a *kiddush* celebration for his twin sister. Neighbors flooded the house with cakes and cookies for the upcoming happy occasions and young girls came over to help set things up.

Since it was summertime, the *shalom zachor* started very late. The last guests left our home after midnight. At 12:45 a.m., my husband and I surveyed the scene of squished cake and chickpeas, spilled soda, two long tables cluttered with used plates, cups, utensils, napkins.... It was a giant mess!

At that moment, we realized just how overwhelmed we were with exhaustion. We had already been up for several nights in a row, taking care of the newborn twins. The thought of cleaning up now was too much. We looked around and wondered how in the world we would cope.

Just then, we were quite surprised to hear a soft knock on the door. It was 1:00 a.m. Who could that be?

We opened up and there stood three sisters we knew from the neighborhood.

"Oh, we were just walking by on our way home from our sister's house, and we thought we would stop in and see if you needed help cleaning up," Sarah said casually, as though there was nothing unusual about them dropping by at one in the morning.

"NEED HELP??!!" We exclaimed with awed relief. "WOW, THANK YOU!!"

God sent us three angels. Amazed to be the recipients of such unexpected kindness, we left the room to their care and collapsed into deep sleep, while the angels were busy in the dining area and kitchen.

When we awoke the next morning, our home looked spotlessly clean.

～∰～

One for the Box

For our children's *bar* and *bat mitzvah* celebrations, we requested, on the invitations, that each guest bring along one item of non-perishable food to be collected at the door and later distributed to families in need, through our local kindness committee in Ra'anana. We arranged decorative wicker collection baskets with colorful signs at the entrance. Thank God, all three were filled with cans, pasta, cereal, rice, and all kinds of other foods by the end of the evening.

We created whimsical charity boxes to place on each table. Each box represented a different type of food bank or fund for families in need. For example, one box was for an organization called "Birthday Angels" created by a wonderful lady, who provides birthday parties to children who would otherwise never have one. We announced that the boxes were available to borrow and pass around for other families' celebrations.

We've made it a family tradition that whenever we have large gatherings such as an anniversary party for grandparents or a Purim banquet, we ask our guests to please "bring something for the box" that we keep outside as a food drop-off point. At first, we were concerned about how people might react to such an unusual request, but the response, thank God, has been overwhelmingly positive.

Right after Purim, we announce on our community's email bulletin board that "the box" is available for dropping off surplus holiday food items that are in closed packages. The response is usually great, thank God. The box is available at all times and gets emptied once a week by the *chesed* committee. I write *"chesed"* on my weekly shopping list so that I won't forget to buy one or two items each week "for the box." When shopping with my kids, I specifically ask them to choose the *chesed* items, so that they'll get in the habit of doing it.

I'm considering answering my Sabbath guests, when they ask "what can I bring?" that they could bring some kind of treat for the box to be distributed the following week. Who knows... I might start a new trend.

A Four-Year-Old's Treat for Soldiers

I just came back with my four-year-old son from a pre-Purim carnival in Gush Etzion, run by our local Shalva group (a daily club for special-needs kids). My son won lots of candy bars as prizes.

As soon as he came home he put them all right into the shoebox he had decorated and prepared in kindergarten to give to soldiers for *mishloach manot* gifts of food for the holiday of Purim. He was so excited. He only ate one and put all the rest away to give to soldiers on Purim.

Jelly Donuts
By C.K., Jerusalem

Last Chanukah, when I entered a large indoor shopping mall in Jerusalem, the security guard at the door was very busy, but he nevertheless, checked my bags and waved me on in a pleasant manner.

Upon making my purchases, I was given a coupon for a free Chanukah jelly donut. I "claimed" my free donut but, instead of eating it myself, on my way out I gave the jelly donut to the security guard who had been so busy but still was so pleasant.

The look of pleasure and surprise on his face was worth a dozen donuts. I wished I had had more to give away. It was a great way to both receive my gift and save myself from consuming the calories!

This year I instituted a slightly different variation: When I went shopping one day, the gentleman who asks for charity outside my local supermarket every Friday morning was sitting at his usual place. I passed by him without giving my usual donation. When I saw him again on my way home from the supermarket, I felt guilty that I had ignored him. So, I stopped at the local snack shop and bought a cup of coffee and next stopped at the local bake shop and bought a jelly donut. I handed both to the gentleman who was seated outside. I told him that I was on a diet, but I hoped that he wasn't.

Just like the security guard, he, too was surprised and gave me a great big smile. His smile was worth more than all the Chanukah donuts. And, hey, look at all of the calories I saved again this year!

How Lucky I Am to Be Able to Share My Love with Others

My friend Yael has a friend named Sarah. She is an artist and speaks only English. Yael thought that because I speak English and run a drama group I might be able to help Sarah sell her paintings.

I was unable to use Sarah's work for the theatre but I realized that my company was doing her good. I have since spent many hours helping her—both with bureaucratic dealings (with the Israeli social services and her doctors) as well as photographing her paintings and writing letters to art galleries.

I invited Sarah to my house during Chanukah to light candles with our family. It was her first time out for a very, very long time, and she made the effort because she trusted me and longed for closeness.

When I drove her home that night she took my hand and thanked me over and over. It made me realize how lucky I am to have the love and kindness of family and friends and to be able to share my love with others.

⌒ᵂᵂᵂᵂ⌒

Happy Chanukah

Reading the kindness emails has really sensitized me to notice opportunities to do kindness. On my way down to the Western Wall, I always see the same man sitting next to the stairs selling *yarmulkes*. He's always there—when it's freezing cold and also when it's extremely hot. I always felt bad for him, but I never knew what to do about it. One of the kindness emails, however, gave me an idea. The last time I saw him, I bought a cup of tea and a donut and handed it to him with a smile, and just said "Happy Chanukah."

⌒ᵂᵂᵂᵂ⌒

Oxygen

My son is oxygen-dependent. Lately, he has needed larger quantities than usual. One night, when we found ourselves running low, we borrowed from a neighbor whose son was also oxygen-dependent. We had asked them several times if they had enough tanks for their own son before we took the tanks. We were under pressure to refill our stock, since Monday evening was the beginning of the holiday of *Rosh Hashanah*.

Sunday evening, the technician arrived. He asked us gently not to borrow again from that neighbor, explaining that despite what she said, she had no spare after giving us hers. "She is so kind, she would never say no," explained the bareheaded earring-wearing deliveryman. "If you are ever stuck, call me on my cell phone. I always have tanks in the car, and I live in Jerusalem."

He started to bring in our tanks. "By the way, I know you are religious, so I brought you extra small tanks, so you can take your son to synagogue to hear *shofar.*"

We found out later that the neighbor with the seriously ill child made a point of asking the technician to provide us with more oxygen. The fact that she had the time to consider the needs of another when her own situation was so difficult was touching. The technician, too, was able to consider our needs from our perspective—an absolute prerequisite for true kindness.

Teaching by Example

Charity collectors come knocking on doors in our community daily, as we are known to be a giving community. Sometimes two people even show up at the same time. It is hard to give a lot to everyone, because there are so many, but we always like to give at least something.

My husband, in addition to giving money, always asks the person if they'd like a drink or something to eat. He says they must be so tired from going house to house. Most people are too shy to accept, but occasionally they agree and are very appreciative.

We often give money to our young children to hand over to

the person collecting charity, to help train them from a young age to give charity. Tonight, the day before *Rosh Hashanah* as we gave my five-year-old the money to give to the person at the door, my eldest daughter said, "Don't forget to give him a big Happy New Year wish!"

It is important not just to give money—a drink and a good wish also go a long way.

───※───

The First Hair Cut

Satellite photos of Israel taken during one night every spring show the country ablaze with bonfires. That night is the mystical holiday of Lag B'Omer, the anniversary of the death of Rabbi Shimon Bar Yocahi, author of the Kabalistic work known as the *Zohar*. A popular custom on Lag B'Omer is that parents cut the hair of their three-year-old sons for the first time during a celebration called *chalakah* (in Hebrew) or *upsherin* (in Yiddish).

One of my best friends had a wedding to go on the night of Lag B'Omer and a *chalakah* celebration to make for her son the next day. I offered to take her three-year-old and her five-year-old for the night of the wedding. They played with my children and ate with us. After dinner I put them to bed. The next day I got them dressed and ready before sending them all home.

Aside from it being an act of kindness to her and her kids, it was great fun for all and a really nice special treat for their "day off" on Lag Ba'Omer! I came to the *chalakah* with my husband's professional camera and shot two rolls of film for them, to spare them the expense of buying a good camera or hiring a photographer just to take a few candid shots.

A True Miracle from Heaven

Several years ago our family spent Passover in a new community which is now called Tal Menashe. We went there to help the residents conduct communal prayers because many of the young families had left Tal Menashe to spend the holidays with their parents.

Our son Ari was in the army down south in Gaza. He was told that he wouldn't get out for the *seder*. At 2:00 p.m. on the afternoon before the *seder* night, the army gave him permission to go home. Since Jewish law forbids travel on the first night of Passover and it was very late in the day, he figured he would hitchhike as far as he could before the holiday and then find a place to stay with friends in the area where he got to.

As soon as he left the army base he got a ride with another soldier. The soldier, who was driving a brand new luxury car with a cell phone in it (something unusual eleven years ago), asked Ari where he had to go. The driver called his mother right away and asked her if he could lend their car to Ari—a total stranger—so that Ari could get home in time for the *seder*.

His mother immediately agreed and asked to speak to Ari. She asked him for his mother's phone number so she could call her and give her the good news that he would be with his family for the *seder*. When Ari told her his name and my name, she realized that the soldier her son had picked up was a distant cousin. We didn't live close to one another so the children didn't recognize each other. The soldier and his mother did a wonderful act of kindness without knowing that they were doing it for a relative.

The wonderful feeling of happiness when Ari came racing up to the community as the men were going to synagogue is something I will treasure forever.

Everyone Pitched In

With Passover drawing near, I dreamed about going away to a hotel... no major cleaning, no cooking, no baking, no dishes to wash, no piles of *matzah* crumbs to sweep from the floor....

But before I knew it, as the holiday approached, I found myself planning for a *seder* of twenty-four people, including family, friends, and students from overseas. Everyone was looking forward to it with excitement, including me! Here's why:

The students volunteered to help clean the house and cook. My children cleaned the closets, drawers and shelves in their rooms. My son planned to be home all week to help with heavy housework and errands. My husband assured me that he would make sure all the work would get done early. He asked me to promise not to stay up late at night preparing for Passover so I would be able to enjoy the *seder*. And I did!

✍

What Would It Take for Me to Have to Go Door to Door?

With Passover coming, Jewish homemakers everywhere are busy preparing for the holiday.

As before every holiday, our neighborhood attracts many people who go door to door collecting charity. In my hurry to complete my work without interruption, I often felt annoyed at these charity collectors for ringing the doorbell and taking me away from whatever I was doing. Then I'd have to scrape together money from my wallet, kitchen drawer, desk top, or wherever else I could find it.

Recently, I reversed my perspective. I have learned to come to see each of these people as a gift, because they have come to teach me something. I also realized that it is a blessing to be able to be on the giving end, and if I give with a smile and an open heart, God will make sure I have enough to give.

In my quest to relate to these people with kindness and respect, I thought to myself once, "What would it take for me to have to go door to door to ask people for financial assistance...."

Now I often listen to someone's story, sympathize with his hardship, and offer him a drink. Sometimes someone is collecting for another family member, perhaps to marry off a child or to pay for an operation. Often the person gives me a blessing for health and good things.

It feels a whole lot better to begin the holiday with the good feeling that I related lovingly to each person who crossed my doorstep.

※

Visitors to Israel

※

A Birthday Celebration with Soldiers

I planned to be in Jerusalem for my 55th, 58th and 59th birthdays. I had friends to celebrate my birthday with me on the first two times. But on the last trip, they were busy that day. It felt sad to be alone on my birthday and I wanted to do some kind of celebrating.

When I saw a soldier outside the Central Bus Station the day before my birthday, I asked her if she could find a dozen soldiers that would like a free meal at a restaurant of their choice so I would have someone to be with on my birthday. We exchanged cell phone numbers and she said she would call the next day. She called and said that her lieutenant told her it was not permissible because it would be a gratuity and that was not acceptable.

Feeling sad and lonely, I went to my favorite shish kabob place on Ben Yehuda Street and ordered my birthday meal. When two solders walked in, I went over to the owner and told him to put their meals on my bill. They looked surprised but happy when the owner told them that it was my treat to them on my birthday.

Mid-way through their meals, an IDF jeep with flashing blue lights came by and one of the soldiers raced out. I felt really sad that his meal was getting cold but this is how life is in Israel. Ten minutes later he came back with a bouquet of flowers and a birthday card. I was in tears, tears of happiness that someone would do that for a stranger.

Since that memorable day, every time I eat at that restaurant, I leave 100 shekels ($25) with the manager and ask him to treat soldiers who come in. I will never know who the soldiers are that enjoy these meals and they will never know who is paying their bill, but I believe it is important to say "Thank You" to soldiers who seldom earn enough to eat in a restaurant. It is my way of repaying the kindness to the soldiers who gave me such a special, wonderful 59th birthday in Israel.

That birthday meal was such a blessing, the kindness of strangers took away my lonely feelings. It was a fantastic highlight and I am pleased to share it in the hope that others will feel inclined to do the same.

We contacted the author three years after she wrote the story. Her update is below:

I had forgotten about this story which appeared in the *Daily Dose of Kindness* email, until one day three years later. As my birthday was approaching, I received an email requesting my permission to print the story in a book. Since I was not going to be in Israel for my birthday, I sent the money with a friend. An email and a suggestion becomes a yearly tradition of thanking soldiers for their courage and responsibility.

Would You Like Some Help?

A few years ago during my trip to Israel, I was carrying about forty books in plastic bags from Meah Shearim to the Sheraton Hotel. The walk seemed like it was taking forever, I was perspiring and my shoulders ached greatly. When I was about half way there, I put the bags down to rest for a moment.

A young man approached me and asked me where I was headed. "To the Sheraton," I replied. "I am going there as well; would you like some help?" he asked.

He carried half my load the rest of the way and all the way up to my hotel room. I thanked him for his kindness and he left. I wondered whether I would ever see him again.

About five months later I went to Miami for school. One Friday afternoon a car pulled up in front of my apartment. A young man stepped out; he seemed to be confused or lost. I ran to greet him, as I always try to do whenever anyone comes. He told me he was lost and he would not be able to get home in time for the Sabbath. I brought him up to my apartment and gave him a bed in my spare room.

I kept looking at him over and over again. I couldn't figure out where I knew him from. I began asking him, "Do I know you from here?" "From there?" The response was always negative.

As I prepared for the Sabbath it dawned on me. He was the guy who helped me on that Jerusalem street. I finally had a chance to repay him.

Help Getting to Israel

A friend of mine called to ask if I knew people who could help with a special financial need. A young person had been planning to go to Israel to study for a year. He had hoped to have money for airfare, but wasn't able to earn or borrow the money in time to buy tickets together with his friends. The airfare was due the following day.

I gave my friend names of a few people that might be able to help. My friend let me know the next day that not only had one of those people come through, but he had taken care of wiring the money immediately to the people collecting the funds for all the tickets.

Better Than Jewelry

Last week, while on a visit to Israel, I saw a ring I really liked which cost about $700. I wasn't sure I wanted to spend that much on a ring, so I did not buy it. That same day we went to a non-profit organization called "Pitchon Lev" in Carmiel. The organization feeds about 1,500 hungry families a week. After a tour of the place I knew why I did not buy that ring. I took out the $700 and gave it to them to buy food for the hungry. It made me feel better than having another ring.

Only Things Made in Israel

On my last trip to visit family in Israel, I did not bring any gifts from America. Instead, I bought all my gifts in Israel and only things "made in Israel." And I got great bargains!

Since I have returned to the United States, I still buy everything from Israel. All my Purim *mishloach manot* (gifts of food) both for Israel and here came from vendors in Israel.

It feels good to shop for goods made in Israel while I am in the United States. It is one small thing that I can do to help the Israeli economy and all of the people who live in Israel.

Sharing Another's Pain

I was visiting Israel a few weeks ago and stopped to pray at King David's Tomb. The building is usually gated up, but a wonderful righteous woman had come that day to sweep up the carpet and leave flowers for the Sabbath.

I love saying Psalms, which were largely written by King David, and have always felt "very close" to him. I had a lot on my mind and the next thing I knew, I was in the building crying hysterically. I just kept crying and crying letting out all of my pain.

After the guard closed the gate, I stepped back outside the building and sat on the stairs of the courtyard and continued crying and praying. Suddenly, a man approached me with a glass of wine and some cake. I had been oblivious to the fact that a family was celebrating an *upsherin* a few feet away.

The man told me that the Sabbath was coming and that God had certainly heard all of my prayers and had taken all of my tears up to Heaven and that everything would be alright.

After he gave me the food, he asked me to come join in his family's celebration. I was stunned to say the least and it got me to stop crying and instead to just smile and say, "Who is like your People Israel?"

This stranger had witnessed my pain and wanted to help me smile again. I was so grateful and so touched. I took out some candy that I had in my purse and gave it to his children who smiled back at me.

What a wonderful act of kindness we can do when we notice and try to share another's pain.

A Wonderful Way to Begin a Month in Israel

In my shared taxi from Ben Gurion Airport to Jerusalem last night, a religious woman was saying how she avoids newspapers, news and world events because everything is just negative. While I had to agree, I told her about these stories going out in emails to thousands daily and how much email subscribers around the world have gained from your contribution to the world based on your tragic loss.

Toward the end of the journey, she said that she is always the last one to be dropped off because she lives in the Old City. I asked her if she'd like to be dropped off before us, knowing how I'd love to drive through the Old City on our first night back to Israel. Both the driver and my husband agreed and excitedly we headed in. The kids were thrilled and I was ecstatic! What a wonderful way to begin a month in Israel!

Your Children Need to See More Than Their Father Writing A Check

The mother of a young man injured in the December 2001 bombing on Ben Yehuda Street called me at KIDS FOR KIDS, requesting a small fridge for her son's hospital room. I knew the rehabilitation ward at Hadassah, Mt. Scopus had public refrigerators in all the wards, so I questioned her request.

She answered, "When I bring my son, Sharon, food for the Sabbath, the Arab orderlies steal the food." My heart was broken. Sharon had barely survived the bombing, sustaining hundreds of shrapnel wounds as well as an inoperable nail in his brain. He was in a coma for months. His recovery was a miracle in itself, and now this. I promised his mother we would find the funds for the fridge.

A week later, Dr. Goldstein, from Miami, Florida walked into my office. Like many tourists visiting Israel for a short time, he was looking for a way to help out victims of terror and possibly get his children involved in the *mitzvah* as well. We talked about some different ideas, but nothing seemed to fit. Then it hit me—I told him about the refrigerator for Sharon.

On the spot, Dr. Goldstein pulled out his checkbook and wrote out the check. "That's not enough," I said with a smile. "Your children need to see more than their father writing a check. Meet me with your family tomorrow at the hospital, and you and your family will present the fridge to Sharon personally. That's the greatest lesson you can teach your children!"

We met the next afternoon at the hospital. It was quite an emotional scene. After stories were told and blessings exchanged, invitations to children's weddings were proffered with teary eyes.

But what impressed me the most was what I have seen time after time—we thought we came to help Sharon and his family, but in the end, Sharon and his mother gave us back so much more. The constant care and dedication to her son, daily for fourteen months, her positive attitude, and her joy for life were so incredibly inspiring and uplifting.

We left with a deeper appreciation for the strength of a Jewish mother and the compassion that gets the Jewish People through these troubled times.

Outside Israel

Kindness in Amman

Three years after I immigrated to Israel and became an Israeli citizen, I realized that being in the garment industry in Israel means traveling to Jordan. At first it seemed a bit scary, but it really isn't scary or dangerous.

During one of my trips, I found myself in Amman, Jordan during a giant snowfall—I couldn't leave to get back to Israel—we were snowed in. I must admit it was a little frightening being stuck in a hotel for two days not knowing when the roads would open again.

I finally was able to get a taxi that was willing to take me to the airport. On the way, we were about to pass a family of four—Mom, Dad and two little kids—just about in the middle of the road—walking amidst all the snow.

I told the driver to stop. If they're going in our direction, why not stop and give them a lift? Sure enough they were going in our direction. They were so pleased that I stopped for them. And boy were they ever surprised that an Israeli/American had offered up this act of kindness in the middle of Amman.

⌒⫘⊷

In The Footsteps of Abraham

Over the last two years, I have had to travel frequently for business to South Africa. Each trip has involved at least one Sabbath stay over, and in most cases also a frantic rush after the Sabbath to catch the Saturday night flight back to Israel.

Families who did not know me before (I made contact via friends in Israel) have time after time put me up for the Sabbath, taken me to the airport, sometimes collected me from the airport after doing a Friday advance check-in, taken me on to their friends (thus widening the kindness circle), and generally made me feel at home in what would otherwise have been a stressful and perhaps miserable Sabbath experience.

They did all of these things with the full knowledge that I am unlikely to be able to adequately reciprocate. If they would come to Israel they would not be faced with the same problems.

The *Torah* teaches us the importance of the *mitzvah* of welcoming guests from the story of Abraham. I have had the privilege to be on the receiving end of this *mitzvah* time and time again, and to learn the *mitzvah*'s practical importance.

─✦─

Life is too short to Waste It on Getting Angry

After living in Israel for three years during the Intifada, I know how precious every minute truly is. I make it a point to tell everyone I love, that I love them each time we speak, email or see each other.

I have learned that nothing is worth getting upset over or angry about—*nothing!*

Nothing is worth yelling at another person.

Life is too short to waste it on getting angry and causing myself and others bad feelings. As I once heard, "Don't sweat the small stuff, and it's ALL small stuff."

I do several things to spread acts of kindness each day. I greet every person with a smile on my face and a kind "Hello." I make sure the tone of my voice is pleasing and not cold, annoyed or unkind.

I was helped over and over again by so many kind and generous people when I lived in Israel. I feel that now I can "pay back" these acts of kindness. I see many elderly people walking long distances to and from local stores each day. I love to stop, help them carry their bags to their destination, or if I am driving, to help get their bags into my car and drop them off at their doorstep, regardless of whether it's on my way or not. I love being able to show them that the younger generation really does care and honor them.

I also love helping the many *yeshiva* students I see at grocery stores who need a ride back to school or to their Sabbath host's homes. I have met so many wonderful people that I would never have met otherwise. These small acts make a huge difference to those I am helping, but in the end, it is I who is moved and changed the most by these experiences.

~~~

One Act of Kindness Deserves Another

My husband had just dropped me off at the airport when two men, looking like rabbis, stopped me and asked in Hebrew if I spoke Hebrew. They told me their destination and it happened to be the city I was flying into. They would then have to take a bus to the city of their destination. Since I had checked in at the curb and they had to go inside and stand on line, I went up front and waited with them for their turn at the ticket counter.

The agent directing "traffic" at the ticket counter asked what I was doing, so I told her I was the translator for the "rabbis." She asked to see my boarding pass and immediately wrote on it, 'BOARDS FIRST." After the rabbis were checked in, she took back my boarding pass and wrote: "FOR 3 PASSENGERS." She told me "one act of kindness deserves another." When we landed I made sure they got on the right bus to connect to their destination.

⤝※⤸

Yossi's Heart
By Abraham J. Twerski, M.D.

Yossi was born with a defective heart. His parents were advised that he would need an operation when he turned seven and that the operation was best done in America.

Yossi's parents, both Israelis, knew no one in America, so when the time came a mutual friend put them in touch with me and I found a medical center in Pittsburgh, where I live, where the surgery could be performed. Several months later Yossi and his parents arrived.

Neither Yossi nor his parents understood a single word of English so I put out the word in the Pittsburgh community for anyone who spoke Hebrew to contact me. Twenty-nine people volunteered and I contacted all of them for an emergency meeting.

At this meeting I explained the predicament. Yossi would be hospitalized for at least two weeks and it was absolutely essential that an interpreter be available at all times. There was no way he could make himself understood to the staff. I asked people to volunteer several hours of their time to be in attendance and we arranged a schedule that covered twenty-four hours a day for two weeks. Each person had an assigned time, and we agreed that one person would not leave until the next arrived.

The plan operated like clockwork. Yossi and his parents were never left alone and not only was there effective interpretation, but the family also received the support of interested people. The postoperative period was not without many anxious moments and Yossi's parents swear that without the moral support of so many friends, they could never have survived it.

The entire hospital staff was impressed by this community cooperation and devotion and when Yossi was discharged the surgeon waived his bill! The family had no insurance coverage and the hospital wrote off whatever they could and gave them the lowest rate. This was paid through donations made by friends of the small community that had sprung up around Yossi.

Before Yossi left for home a gala party was held, attended by the volunteers, contributors, surgeon and other members of the hospital staff. Tearful good-byes were said, there was much embracing, lots of people gave of themselves and got back this: they had helped save a little boy. Along the way each one discovered qualities inside that might never have been tapped if not for Yossi. On top of this many friendships had been formed during this period and these people who had not known each other became close friends, having worked for a common cause.

Six years later on a visit to Israel I made a surprise visit to Yossi, but he wasn't home: he was playing basketball! I went to the playground and could not stop my tears of joy when I saw the robust little boy who had once been so hampered by illness playing a game of hoops. On my return to Pittsburgh I contacted the participants in Yossi's operation for a reunion and we all bonded again as we shared the news. One man originally had been reluctant to help because he was terrified of hospitals. Now he relayed that he no longer hesitated to visit friends when they were ill; he had gotten over a phobia that had controlled him. It's twenty years later. Yossi is happily married and has a child. He sends cards twice a year which we circulate. In this way the group stays in touch and when a member needs help or wants to share happiness we are there.

What we did for Yossi pales in comparison to what Yossi did for us. Each of us is stronger as a result of this event. That is the power of goodness.

Rabbi Abraham J. Twersky is the founder of the Gateway Rehabilitation System. This article is reprinted from "Do Unto Others: How Good Deeds Can Change Your Life."

A Secret Kindness

I returned last Wednesday after spending two weeks studying at a *yeshiva* in Jerusalem's Old City. It was like heaven on earth. One of the things we discussed was a ten-step daily checklist for doing a Spiritual Accounting, developed by Rabbi Avigdor Miller. One of the steps was to make sure to do a "secret kindness" every day in order to train ourselves to strip away any sense of ego as a motivating factor in doing kindness. I started practicing this by doing small things like clearing away garbage that people leave behind and making sure when I park my car in the street that I leave enough room for someone to park behind me.

⟨⟨⟨

She Comes from Israel, Where Everyone Is Always Ready to Help Someone Else in Need

I had just gone shopping in Manhattan and was returning home to Queens on the F train. After a few stops, I noticed a woman got on at the other end of the car, and was excitedly gesticulating to someone on the subway platform, calling out rather inarticulately as the train pulled out of the station. It was obvious that something was wrong with the big woman and with her situation.

A small, dark woman approached her and began to talk to her. When the train stopped at the next station, they both got off and went to speak to the conductor. Then we could hear the conductor speaking over what was probably his radio.

The train waited as a female and a male police officer approached the two women. Then the small, dark passenger got back on the train and, through the window, I saw the big woman walking quietly with the police officers.

I pieced together what I thought had occurred. The big woman seemed to be retarded and must have gotten separated from her companion. The small, dark woman stepped in to help her solve her problem.

I got out of my seat and went to compliment her for what she had done. The small woman explained that the big woman had been separated from her mother when the door closed quickly after she boarded. She was obviously distressed, and the small woman felt she had to try to help her.

She went on to explain that she comes from Israel, where everyone is always ready to help someone else in need. *"Kol hakavod"* (you performed an honorable deed), I told her, as she looked at me in surprise.

Our conversation continued in Hebrew. She was anxious to get home to pick up her young son from school, yet she took the time to perform this kind deed. She said that she was disappointed to observe that Americans don't seem to help each other the way Israeli's are accustomed to. I agreed.

How proud I felt of this young Israeli, in the U.S. for just five years. How proud I felt to be an Israeli, too.

Israel Responds
to Terror

Unmasking the REAL Israel
By Stewart M. Weiss

Will the real Israeli please stand up? Is it the gruff, tough ruffian who cuts you off in traffic, endangering life and limb—his and yours—for the sake of one car-length? Is it the rude and pushy person who mysteriously appears at the bank or post office—just as you are about to finally advance to the clerk—and cavalierly informs you, "I was here."

Or is it the driver who pulls off the road to help you with the baby carriage, all the while telling you what a cute baby you have; or the supermarket clerk who runs down the street chasing you to return the ten shekels change you forgot when you checked out?

Over the last month, since our son Ari was killed in battle in Nablus, I have had the opportunity to encounter the Israeli, and the Israel, you never—or rarely—see; certainly the Israel you almost never read about. It is, I can report, an Israeli with a huge heart, a towering soul, and an inner desire to do good.

From the moment we received the horrendous news about our valiant soldier, we were shielded in a protective bubble of love and care that defies description. Within minutes of the army's dreaded knock on our front door, hundreds of friends took it upon themselves to attend to our every need, from providing three meals a day, to cleaning our house, to seeing to it that we are never alone.

The entire Ra'anana community, led by Israel's most popular mayor, Zev Bielski, became mother hens and big brothers who took us under their wing and stood by our side.

From near and far came amazing gestures of sympathy and solidarity: The local Starbucks—the only kosher Starbucks in the world!—sent dozens of specialty coffees to our home each day during the week of mourning. A neighborhood synagogue set up a "mobile sanctuary" in our living room so we could pray at home.

A jeweler in Jerusalem took the bullet casings used in the "twenty-one-gun salute" to Ari at his funeral and made out of them, at no cost, commemorative rings for all the family. A ten-year-old boy from Hashmonaim, who watched the funeral on TV, saw our ten-year-old wearing a torn shirt (as required by Jewish law) and sent him a new T-shirt in the mail. Christians from Montana sent dolls to all the children.

We were overwhelmed with acts of kindness, and generosity of the spirit, from people we had never met before. Dozens came to visit us, expressing solidarity through the beautiful Hebrew expression, "I share in your pain." Included among them, alas, were many who had themselves been victims of the Palestinian Terror War against the Jewish People. They, more than anyone, know what it means to suffer and to sacrifice for this great nation of Israel. Politicians came, too, to let us know we were not alone. President Moshe Katsav sat with our nine-year-old daughter and animatedly asked her about school. Natan and Avital Sharansky cried with us and invited us to Sabbath dinner at their home. Effie Eitam hailed our son as a hero and left his home number in case we needed to call.

Most impressive of all was the IDF (Israel Defense Forces). They mobilized into "battle mode" to guard and guide us. Ari's unit—sent letters by their commanding officer "ordering" them to now make us part of their own families—surrounded us like a wall of green.

Battle-trained generals came to sit with us, and several were even caught shedding a tear. The Chief of General Staff, Moshe Ya'alon, spent an hour telling us how many lives had been saved by Ari's final mission.

I look out on all of this love, all of these expressions of unsolicited kindness, and I am absolutely convinced that we are a nation like no other.

And I know that Ari—whose death has sparked such an outpouring of positive emotion around the world—did not die in vain.

Stewart M. Weiss is director of the Jewish Outreach Center of Ra'anana.

⁓

Raise Your Spirits

When things were at an all-time low here, and we were all losing friends and family members on a daily basis, a very dear friend of mine, Sharon Katz, had a dream—a summer stock women's theatre group. The group was named the "Efrat/Gush Etzion Raise Your Spirits Summer Stock Company."

The group's goal was, and remains, to raise everyone's spirits and also to provide financial support to programs that assist victims of terror and provide other critical needs. The first musical, "Joseph," was great. Although we weren't living here yet, I saw it several times while we were visiting. It was during a period when I was mourning the loss of many close friends.

We had just arrived from America before the second play, "Esther," started. I worked on the technical side of the production. In "Noah," I had a small acting part and also worked on makeup and backstage.

"Raise Your Spirits" has helped many of us in many ways. The theatre group has entertained thousands of women here in Gush Etzion and even traveled to Gush Katif (Gaza) to perform. The groups plans to take the next show, "Ruth & Naomi," to the women of Gush Katif, wherever they are today.

Unity—Boy, Does It Feel Good!

Since my family arrived in Israel, we have been devastated by the terror. It was just too much to bear. When Tali Hatuel, her unborn child and her four young daughters were murdered, I knew I could not just go on without some drastic action.

I called all of my friends and neighbors. Many of these women were going through the ever too common trauma of feeling the pain but feeling helpless and violated. I was angry at everyone. I became so depressed that a friend of mine, who is very spiritual, told me I had reached a dead-end completely.

I knew something must be done this time. So I called an emergency meeting and boy, was I ready to change the world. Somehow at this meeting of unity on the eve of Tali's *shloshim* (communal spiritual gathering held thirty days after a person's death), my anger was transformed into something beautiful.

On that night thirty-five women came to honor Tali and

IMACHDUT was born! On that night we created an organization to create unity within us so that fear won't have power to harm us.

Out of that act of giving came so much love and healing. Our emblem became a healing heart and our motto: "IMACHDUT... healing us all, one heart at a time." Our mission: to promote the *mitzvah* of loving our neighbor as ourselves.

We get together every *Rosh Chodesh* (the first day of the Jewish month). At these meetings we learn how to be loving and non-judgmental and respectful of others' differences and to honor the principals of unity.

We continue spreading love and acceptance in our neighborhood and all I can say is "Boy, does it feel so good!!!"

❧❧❧

Tribute to Adva Fisher

While it is easy to see how happiness can make the world better, it is often harder to understand how tears can.

This story is about Adva Fisher, who was killed in the terrorist attack at Tzomet Geha. She was studying at a school in the city of Tzefat where my daughter had the merit of being her roommate.

Adva was always looking to do *mitzvahs*, but the following story tells about the humility and modesty that accompanied her.

In addition to working twice a week with a young immigrant from a broken home and making a serious contribution in a very short time, Adva volunteered daily at a soup kitchen in Tzefat.

She begged the manager of the soup kitchen to give her a key so that she could go in often, and work when no one was around. The manager didn't want to give her a key, but she wouldn't let up until he gave in.

She would go in every day to clean the place up, and mop the floors without anyone watching her. No one even knows the true amount of time she spent there, since she did this with no one around.

When her mother saw the key lying around with a sticker on it, she asked Adva what the key was for, but Adva made up a cover story so that even her own mother wouldn't know the extent of her *mitzvahs*. It was only after her death, when the manager of the soup kitchen wrote a three-page letter describing how special she was, that her family discovered what that key was for.

The soup kitchen also was available to poor couples getting married, and Adva would always get up early on those days to personally decorate the hall, and make it more of a wedding atmosphere for these couples who could only afford a soup kitchen for their wedding. She did this as well with no one watching

The girls who stayed at the school for the Sabbath would always make *challah*. Adva saw how hard they worked and wanted to make it a bit easier for them. She heard about an electric flour sifter and took out 180 shekel ($45) from her bank account in order to buy it as a gift for them. (After her death, her parents took the money that she set aside, added another

180 shekel of their money, and purchased two electric sifters to give the girls at the school. They asked the girls to always think of Adva when they make *challahs*.)

Adva filled her life with acts of kindness and made the world better during her too short life.

Such Wonderful Opportunities

After reading an article about a paragon of kindness who was recently killed in a terrorist attack, and a woman who did not have the chance to tell her how special she was, I started tracking down one of my influential teachers from third grade. I finally got her number in the U.S.

When I called just to thank her for being such a special teacher, she was so thankful. She said that elderly people get very lonely, and these types of calls mean so much to her.

She was especially appreciative that I called from Israel. She told me she keeps track of all her students and she knew exactly where I live, what my husband does, what was going on with all my siblings, and she even remembered my address in Boston.

If I would have known how important it was to make this call, I would have done so years ago. A phone call can be a very powerful act of kindness. It's so easy and so quick. Such wonderful opportunities should not be missed.

⌒≈≀≀≀≀≀⌒

Someday Peace Will Be Made with a Human Gesture

Our son Gedaliah was a soldier in the Israel Defense Forces. He served as a commander of recruits, and also as radio man for the IDF "Golani" front line troops. Gedaliah was killed in Jenin after seven consecutive days and nights of battle against terrorists. He was just twenty-one years old.

He was a gentle and good-natured young man. The following act of kindness was one of several which he performed during the heavy battles against terrorists, when every second of time lost might cause the death or wounding of the Israeli forces.

A civilian Palestinian family were hosting and living together in one house with terrorists. The terrorists were on the run and went into hiding in one of the many rooms in the house. The civilian family, a mother and father and five very young children, was discovered huddled in a corner of a room by the Israeli forces that entered the house in search of terrorists.

The family was absolutely frozen in fear. They were sure that when the soldiers came in, they would be executed, since they had been drilled to believe that Jews are evil and cruel. The Israel forces commander who spoke Arabic told the family to immediately vacate the building for their own safety. He pointed them towards the back door and the path that led straight down to the mosque, where food and shelter and basic commodities had been set up by the army to receive the civilians.

The family remained frozen in place. They were simply paralyzed from fear, and waited to be shot to death. Our son, serving with the advance command, Staff Sergeant Gedaliah, saw that the family was unable to obey any rational talk. He stepped forward, bent down over the mother, and handed her a chocolate cake from his pouch—a cake he had been saving for his comrades, who had had almost no fresh food in the past twenty-four hours, as food supplies were not moving up to the front lines.

The soldiers had seen that cake and were waiting out the prescribed time between eating meat and milk, in keeping with Jewish dietary law. They had eaten canned meat for breakfast, to relieve the weight in their pouches and were looking forward to eating that cake towards evening, to relieve their hunger.

When Gedaliah pulled out the cake and handed it over to the mother of the family, she reached out and took it, in disbelief, and then she suddenly understood. After breaking off a few pieces of cake for the children, she and her husband, now understanding that no harm was meant towards them, got up off the floor, gathered their young ones in their arms, and taking the directions given, walked out of the building.

Someday, peace will be made with a human gesture, like that, but on a grander scale. May the People of Israel be rejuvenated, and restored to our ancient heritage and to our faith in the God of Israel.

For information about Yad Gedaliah, a charity set up in memory of Gedaliah, see the list of kindness organizations at the end of this book, page 272.

The Cost of Peace: Tragedy in Gaza

Bikes for Kids

Imagine, if you can, being evicted from your home by the government, in an effort to secure peace. Imagine leaving the only home you've ever known, your town, your friends, your place of work, knowing that the entire place would be destroyed. Imagine entire families, parents and children, being uprooted from their homes and sent off to hotels and guest houses with a small bag, and no idea of how long they will be "homeless."

This actually happened to thousands of ordinary citizens of Israel's Gush Katif (Gaza) in the summer of August 2005. When they were removed from their homes they were assured by the government that there was a "solution for each settler," in the way of permanent housing. They took minimal belongings, assuming that since they were assured the government was providing housing, they would soon be given this permanent housing and thus be able to retrieve their own belongings from storage.

One such woman told me that she took articles for the holiday of *Sukkot* (which is in the early fall) but it never occurred to her that she would need to take her religious articles for *Purim* as well (a holiday which falls in the spring)! As a nation for the most part remained impassive, these uprooted citizens spent an average of nine months in hotel rooms and guests houses around the country. Large families of six, seven and even ten children, living in two or three hotel rooms, with no ability to have a family meal or even privacy for nine months! Nine months without any sense of normalcy. Nine months of mourning their entire community and way of life.

After nine months the "temporary housing" promised by the government was ready, almost. These good citizens left their first (or for some, second) temporary dwelling to move to their next temporary dwelling, a trailer-like structure, much, much smaller than the homes they owned. These caravans (mobile homes), for the most part, cannot contain all of their belongings and are poorly built. But for these courageous citizens, they are a home after nine months of homelessness. And so they decorate them proudly and welcome guests into them happily. Because at least, finally, they can cook their own meals, and decide when their children should go to sleep.

The children though, are another story. Accustomed to blossoming communities, where lovely parks, sports fields and community centers were everywhere, they don't know what to do in the wasteland that has become their new home for the next several years. There is no accommodation for any kind of activities. Until a man by the name of Moshe, who owns a bicycle store in Jerusalem, together with his mother, Esti, had a brainstorm. Many people, who live in their own homes, have assorted bicycles that their own children have outgrown. Moshe began to take them in, fix them up good as new, and donate them to the children of Gush Katif. The idea took off, and people from communities all over Israel started to donate their used bicycles to Moshe's bike shop where they were fixed up and shipped out to the caravan villages for the youth of Gush Katif. As more and more communities heard of this project, Esti started raising funds to purchase more bikes for the Gush Katif kids. A community in the U.S. took upon themselves the former Gush Katif settlement of Morag, and provided for the purchase of a bike for each family there.

The children, as well as their parents, are thrilled. The smiles on their faces when the bikes arrive are incredible. Finally, there is something for them to do in the wasteland they call home. They can be independent again; they can ride outside, and even help their parents by doing errands on their bikes. And as for their parents, the fact that people from all over the world care enough to donate to this project, close to a year after their expulsion from their homes, once again, there is hope.

This story was adapted from Viewpoint, published by the National Council of Young Israel.

The More We Give the More We Have

This story was written before the expulsion from the Gaza Strip.

Reading your quote of the week, (from one of your *Daily Dose of Kindness* emails, "Whoever is eager to donate charity, the Holy One Blessed Be He gives him money"), I felt I had to write to you about how this *Talmudic* statement comes true every day of the week here where I live.

My neighbors and I grow vegetables in greenhouses in Gush Katif. An extraordinary person in the area started collecting a box or two of vegetables from every grower who was willing to give them. Then he prepared beautiful colored packages with a wide variety of vegetables and distributed them discreetly to needy families in the area.

Soon he had more vegetables than he needed since the growers insisted on giving him more, so *he* started working with social services in other cities and distributing his packages there. He enlisted young volunteers to help him with the sorting and packaging.

Soon the schools of advanced *Talmudic* study and charity organizations in these cities started sending people to collect vegetables for their needy families as well.

Before Passover *charity organizations* come from all over the country to get donations of vegetables.

Every farmer in Gush Katif will tell you a proven fact, the more vegetables we give to the needy, the more blessing we have in our produce. Giving charity is a proven formula for success in the farms of Gush Katif.

The author wrote this update after the expulsion:

The story as related is 100% correct, except for one minor correction. It is that Gush Katif no longer physically exists. However, I must tell you that after the expulsion all looked so black. Our houses and our livelihood were destroyed; we lived in hotels for months; it took months till we saw even down payments on compensation; our belongings were in storage containers without ability to access them, and we faced many more difficulties.

One day I said to myself, "I must be looking at this thing wrong because God's world can't be so black."

When we were in Gush Katif I planted seedlings of celery in my greenhouses even on the last day before we were expelled from our home in Netzer Hazani. Many people thought I was crazy because the expulsion was a certainty.

I said "God's help comes like the blink of an eye," so I will plant so if the help comes, God willing, like the blink of an eye, I'll have celery to pick in another two months. I must have blinked because I didn't see the *help*. It didn't happen.

Sure enough when I made this switch in my head, I realized that I had wanted God to do what I wanted. That is, to save my home and agro business and my little piece of the land of Israel that I could put my feet on. But God had other plans.

With eyes wide open, I realized, as I now look back, that there had been amazing *help* all along. People waiting with flowers at every corner as we drove to the Western Wall in dark green army buses when we were taken out of Netzer Hazani—a real help from God.

At 3:00 a.m., over ten thousand wonderful Jews waiting to greet us at the Western Wall, pulling us, who were traumatized and lacking all our physical possessions other than what we could fit in our little backpacks, off the buses, greeting us with flowers, drinks and food, grabbing us to dance with them at the Wall. This was a real help.

I learned that caring gives strength to both the giver and receiver; it causes a chain of kindness that produces endless ripples in all directions.

Giving up a Job to Someone Who Needs It More

Several of the families who were uprooted from their homes, communities and livelihood in Gush Katif, Gaza have moved to our community. I just heard about one of the most remarkable acts of kindness I've ever heard. A young man, who got his first teaching job, gave it up for a man from Gush Katif. He simply stated that the displaced teacher has a large family and needs the job more than he does.

An Ongoing Loan

My husband and I read in *Chicken Soup for the Soul* about a man who "returned" a loan by passing it on to help someone else in need. We have given a few loans like this. It's much easier for someone to accept a loan of money knowing that whenever he is able (in ten or twenty years or more) he can repay it by passing it on to someone else in need.

Two families that we were able to help in this way were evacuated from Gush Katif. Before the evacuation, both couples had jobs and lived comfortably. Afterwards they had neither homes, nor jobs, nor a means to pay for even basic needs.

We hope we were able to help these proud families and also give them hope that one day they too will be on the "giving" end and able to lend to someone else in need.

Another loan we made was to one of my husband's students who was very depressed and was told by his doctor to start regular exercise—preferably swimming. Since this nineteen-year-old did not know how to swim it just added to his frustration.

We loaned him money to take swimming lessons and to regularly exercise. The terms of the loan are as described above. He would never have accepted charity, but he accepted this type of loan, which never has to be paid back, unless he's able. He is now swimming and on the way to recovery.

They Must Give

My family and I spent the Sabbath after the expulsion of Jews from Gush Katif in Ashkelon. We wanted to be in a place where we could help and try to strengthen our heroes who were cruelly expelled.... To where? They still don't know!

At the Sabbath table in one of the hotels (temporary, crowded residences for up to or even longer than five months) one of the former Gush Katif residents rose and said, "Since we've come here, we've been showered by so much love. So many people have come to distribute cakes, flowers and snacks. Since we have too many snacks for ourselves and since we are a community that likes to give, I propose that after Sabbath we go to the nearby Barzilai Hospital and distribute these snacks to the children hospitalized there."

I was dumbfounded! They have no home, no idea where their children will go to school in a few weeks, yet they so much hate being on the receiving end—they must give in order to slowly return to normalcy!

╼❧╾

They Are Not Used to Being on the Receiving End

Lema'an Achai, a local charity organization in Ramat Beit Shemesh has been helping to organize volunteers to help our brothers and sisters who were evicted from their homes in Gush Katif, Gaza. It has been amazing to hear of professionals taking time off from work to spend full days helping these people. Psychologists and social workers have gone to counsel both adults and children. People have gone to a variety of locations to assist in any way possible—packing, unpacking, schlepping, entertaining displaced children, etc.

A handyman recently apologized on a local email list to any customers who had been trying to reach him. He explained that he was temporarily unavailable as he was in Atzmona in Gush Katif, helping former residents dismantle their hothouses so that they could salvage as much as possible to try to rebuild their livelihoods.

The residents of Gush Katif are not used to being on the receiving end. The director of the aforementioned charity organization, which until now has serviced only local Ramat Beit Shemesh residents, said a couple of weeks ago that he asked the truck driver who delivers donated vegetables why that week he only had cucumbers and potatoes when he usually brought so much more than that. The driver replied, "All the other donations used to come from Gush Katif. Tons and tons. Literally ten trucks a day...."

∽≫⊱≺⊰≍∾

1-2-3-4, Lift Off!

Imagine being permanently evacuated from your home with no access to your possessions. This was the situation for many former residents of Gush Katif, Gaza, Israel when the National Council of Young Israel, the umbrella organization for over 150 synagogues throughout North America, coordinated a clothing campaign to help these families. The clothing donations benefited other needy families in Israel. Four lifts of about 1800 boxes each were sent, by boat, to Israel for distribution to the former residents of Gush Katif.

Rabbi Pesach Lerner, Executive Vice President of the National Council of Young Israel, took a personal interest and involvement in this major effort.

"It all started when the National Council of Young Israel received a telephone call from Dr. Daryl Tempkin, from L.A., an individual who has been active in the Gush Katif cause for many years. Daryl informed me that he had heard of the tremendous need for clothing for the Gush Katif refugees. Much of their clothing had been packed in storage containers, and they have no access to it unless they pay storage, rental, and moving costs. The regulations also dictate that when an owner opens a container, it must be emptied. Where does one put a houseful of possessions when living in a hotel or dormitory room or in a tent? Many of the refugees have been relocated to much colder climates and do not even own warm garments.

"Dr. Tempkin had already begun coordinating a clothing drive in Los Angeles. He told me that after the publicity began, hundreds of emails and phone calls were received from Jews on the East Coast. He asked the National Council of Young Israel to spearhead the drive in the metropolitan New York area. Of course, NCYI responded positively, and he directed all of the East Coast inquiries to us.

"One of the emails that we received at the office was from an American, Rabbi Maier Solomon, who has lived in Israel for close to twenty years. Rabbi Solomon told us that he runs a clothing gemach in Jerusalem, and has experience in sending lifts from the United States. He offered his assistance and directed us to his Brooklyn acquaintance, Rafi.

"I met with Rafi, who agreed that the Raphael Chesed Store in Brooklyn, New York, would be the local clothing drop-off point. The clothing would then be stored at his Brooklyn warehouse for preparation for "lift-off." Ads were placed in the Jewish media, emails were sent throughout the metropolitan New York and the tri-state areas, fliers were distributed to local synagogues, and lo and behold, boxes and boxes were dropped off in Flatbush.

"Rafi's generosity has been truly amazing. He offered his truck for pick-ups of local community clothing drives, and suggested parking the truck for a day at a time in certain neighborhoods for more convenient clothing drop-offs. Each time the truck was filled.

"Local clothing campaigns were organized in communities throughout New York and New Jersey. Clothing manufacturers called to donate winter coats. Boxes of clothing were shipped from Houston (TX), Memphis (TN), Brookville, (MA), Silver Spring and Baltimore (MD), Philadelphia (PA), Indiana and places in-between. Local campaigns were coordinated in Boca Raton (FL), Chicago (IL), and Detroit (MI). Inspired by the activities of the National Council of Young Israel, members of the

Toronto Jewish community organized their own clothing lift to Israel.

"To date, four forty-foot lifts containing between 1500-1800 boxes each had arrived in Israel. The New York warehouse has enough boxes to fill a fifth lift, including eighty boxes from the members of the Buffalo (NY) Jewish community, and maybe even a sixth. (Although these lifts are waiting until additional funds are raised to cover the shipping costs).

"As soon as the clothing arrived in Israel, it was sorted by gender and size and brought to a clothing 'store' in a convenient location in Jerusalem so that the former Katifniks could come and take whatever they need for their families. At the same time similar items of winter clothing, sweaters, scarves, children's clothing, men's pants, women's skirts, etc. were packed onto trucks and taken to other locations where the refugees are living. The goal was simply to assist our brothers and sisters, to dress them and keep them warm.

"Who would have expected such a response from all segments of the community? Hassidic Jews in Boro Park, high school kids, a nontraditional synagogue in Queens, communities throughout the United States, and New York clothing manufacturers. The Jewish community is truly blessed!

This story was adapted from Viewpoint, published by the National Council of Young Israel.

◦⧼⧽◦

Purim Story: Anatomy of a Smile
By Sharon Katz

Every month the women of Efrat and Gush Etzion visit a different community around the country, as part of our efforts to show our support for and unity with women of other communities. This year, we have been visiting women from former Gush Katif towns. On a visit to Kfar Nofesh Ashkelon, where families from Moshav Katif and Neve Dekalim are living, the women listened to one another speak about their lives. My friend Judy Rosenstark, who is Efrat's volunteer coordinator for efforts to the Gold, Gates and Shalom Hotels, asked the Gush Katif women if she could help them in some way.

They replied, "While your families might be looking toward Tu B'Shevat right now, we're already worried about Purim. Our children's costumes are in our containers, if they're still wearable. And we can't make anything new even if we wanted to, because we have no sewing machines, no material, nothing to work with."

Judy, in her compassionate way, said, "Don't worry. Efrat will make sure the children of Kfar Nofesh have Purim costumes. How many do you need?" "More than 100!" "No problem," she gulped. So, Judy began scouting for Purim costumes. She asked Efratians to donate their children's lightly used costumes, or to buy an extra one when they went shopping for their own children.

Weeks passed, but costumes only dribbled in, and Judy was worried. She couldn't face the women of Kfar Nofesh who really believed her when she said, "Don't be anxious about it anymore. It's all taken care of."

Enter Young Israel.

One month before, I had written an article about an incredible series of clothing shipments, funded by the National Council of Young Israel, to the people of Gush Katif from Jews all America. I had the opportunity then to interview the Young Israel's Executive Vice President Rabbi Pesach Lerner about the shipments.

I knew he'd want to know that the children of Gush Katif had no Purim costumes. And I asked him for any idea he might have about how I could acquire some.

He responded immediately, "How much are Purim costumes? How many are needed? Can they be bought in bulk? Wholesale? Do we know which kids want them? Where they are? Let's make this story happen—a Purim costume for every kid."

Simultaneously, Judy emailed a family friend, Phil Rosenblatt of the Amazing Savings stores, and asked how much 100 costumes would cost for the children of Gush Katif. Phil replied, "I'll donate eighty. The rest—cost." He got to work immediately looking for folks traveling to Israel who could bring boxes of costumes.

Every day another call came, from Tel Aviv, Ashkelon, Jerusalem. Everyone had boxes from Phil Rosenblatt.

Meanwhile, Rabbi Lerner had gone into action. Four days after my first mention of costumes to him, Rabbi Lerner had already launched a costume campaign in America, got Assemblyman Dov Hikind to speak about it on his radio show, and sent out his first flyer for Kostumes 4 Kids of Katif.

Suddenly our goal had changed. Now, we'd buy and distribute as many costumes as Rabbi Lerner could raise money for.

Looking for a costume supplier, we hooked Rabbi Lerner up with Phil Rosenblatt.

From that moment on, Rabbi Lerner, Phil, Judy and I formed a team with one aim: not just providing Purim costumes for the 132 children of Kfar Nofesh, but as many Gush Katif and Northern Shomron children as possible.

Judy and I scrambled for information from costume distributors throughout the country, and were even planning an all-day trip to importers in Haifa or Holon, when Phil suddenly put us in contact with Vivi, a close-out buyer from Ashdod.

Never having come into contact with the Jews of Gush Katif, Vivi was captured by the enthusiasm of our team, and looked throughout Israel for the best costume deals she could find.

Suddenly in Israel, news of over-run lady bugs and bunny rabbits, cowboys and clowns, pirates and princesses began flowing in. In the U.S., Rabbi Lerner's campaign was in full swing. The rabbi told us that he believed Dov Hikind's appeal on the radio would lead to enough money for 1000 costumes.

Judy began contacting the remnants of every single destroyed town. It was the work of a detective and a CPA. Working day and night, Judy tracked down the location of every single child from Gush Katif and Northern Shomron, and calculated the number of costumes, sizes and genders. Kfar Darom was in Ashkelon, Netzer Chazani was in Ein Tzurim, Chispin, Chafetz Chaim and Kvutzat Yavne. Eli Sinai was in Yad Mordechai. Ganei Tal, Gadid, Gan Or, Atzmona, Neve Dekalim and Katif were in Yad Binyamin. Chomesh and Sanur were in Shavei Shomron and Yitzhar. On and on it went. She kept detailed notes, and found that instead of needing 1000 costumes, in order to outfit every child of Gush Katif (up to ages ten or eleven), we needed more than 2000 costumes. The thousands of older kids couldn't be forgotten either, and they would get accessories, like wacky hats and hair paint.

Rabbi Lerner and Phil Rosenblatt were in New York trying to make the campaign happen. In Israel, Judy and I were nervous. Maybe we could collect 2000 costumes, and even distribute them, but if we made a mistake, and left out any communities or any children, instead of the joy of Purim, there would be the disappointment of an entire group of people.

But our New York counterparts gave us all encouragement. "You can and must do it!!" Phil said, "Getting a costume for each child is a big motivation and goal for all of us. And while money is not unlimited, I don't think we should overlook how important it is for children to celebrate Purim."

Having a costume may not mean more than food or clothing, but for a few days, being able to wear a costume may be more meaningful to each child and his parents, Phil said.

Rabbi Lerner commented, "If we can make 2000 kids forget about the real problems they face, even for just a few minutes, that is a serious *mitzvah*. As you hand out the costumes you will see the smiles, the thanks. Then we will know the truth."

A few days later a giant truck, filled to capacity with costumes and accessories, drove into Efrat and right up to Judy's door. Six women went to work sorting the spacemen, Peter Pans, animals and Mordechai HaYehudis from the kings and queens. In addition to the dozens of types of Israeli costumes, we had the original magnificent animal costumes from Amazing Savings.

The mothers oohed and ahhed, as they packed bags for more than twenty locations. And as they worked, the phone rang a few times with Rabbi Lerner or Phil on the other end, wishing to be part of the exhilaration.

Not one town would be left out, whether it was scattered in hotels or schools around the country, or tucked away in an isolated location, like the Netzarim families in Yevul on the Egyptian border, the cut off-Neve Dekalim families in Netivot, or the Morag families in Tene Omarim, south of Chevron.

Sharon Katz is Editor of VOICES Magazine. This story was adapted from Viewpoint, published by the National Council of Young Israel.

Speedy Delivery

Families from Efrat lined up to deliver the costumes, no matter how far. Judy and I made the first delivery with the same bus that had taken us to Kfar Nofesh a month before. This trip was to the Gush Katif refugee camp Nitzan. We stuffed the bus with dozens of bags filled with costumes for the 605 children there.

Nitzan was a horror—a displacement camp with mud ruts running down streets. I asked a woman how she is. She said, "Thank God, terrible." I said, "Excuse me?" She replied, "You have to thank God for the good as well as the bad."

But when they saw the magnificent costumes, they could not contain their joy from each outfit, as well as the heartwarming notes from the Young Israel.

Rabbi Lerner was overwhelmed with the reception the costumes got. He told us, "The heavens are dancing tonight!!!!!!!" And they were.

Of course, as soon as the word got out that we were actually delivering the costumes, small detached communities and single families began calling. Judy made sure every straggler was included in the campaign, even though she and other friends had to shop again for hundreds of more costumes.

Gush Katif Reactions

Delivering the costumes to the Shalom Hotel, where many families from Neve Dekalim live, Judy spoke to the preschool teacher. The teacher said, "You can't imagine how thrilled the families are! It's not that we don't have costumes. I have gorgeous costumes with my stuff, but who knew that we'd need to take stuff for Purim? I personally brought enough things with me to last through *Sukkot* (in October), but who could have imagined then in August that we'd need to bring our costumes and *Megillat Esther*?"

Judy and I traveled to Ashkelon to deliver costumes to the families from the northern Gaza Strip, Duggit and Nisanit. We were greeted in the parking lot of the community center by lovely women and children. We asked where they were from. "Duggit, but we live here now," and they pointed to the apartment building, evidently in disrepair. One mother said sadly, "It's not good for us here."

Spirits rose as we laid out the costumes and children started trying them on. Something for everyone, and a tremendous variety.

Other mothers delivered costumes throughout the week. Kfar Nofesh finally got their costumes. Some of our friends drove down and brought the boxes to the preschool. They opened up the boxes and bags. The kids had a great time trying on costumes and everyone began to sing and dance. When the

Efrat mother said she had to leave, one child tugged at her skirt and asked with a sad face, "Do I have to take off the costume now and give it back to you? Can't I wear it just a bit longer?" Another boy asked, "Can you come back again next week so we can do this again?" When she explained that the costumes were theirs to keep the kids were in astounded. "Really? Ours?" They simply couldn't believe it.

Writer Toby Klein Greenwald is the grandmother of three Atzmona children now living in Sha'al Vim. After picking up her grandchildren's costumes from our campaign, she wrote, "When I opened the bag and saw the three outfits, princess-like dresses for five-year-old Tehila and three-year-old Shir-el, and a little clown suit and hat for almost one-year-old Oz Naftali, I got all choked up and emotional."

"My daughter could have asked me to help her make costumes... but she chose to be part of the Purim 'love fest' of costumes, like her friends. It was then that I realized the extent to which the Purim costume project was not about money, or about an afternoon at the sewing machine; it was about the Nation of Israel sharing their love with the beloved extraordinary people of Gush Katif."

The Kostumes 4 Kids of Katif has completed its mission, thank God—ultimately outfitting 2500 elementary school children with bright happy costumes, giving them a reason to smile, and the ability to feel (for two days at least) that they are just regular kids enjoying a holiday like everyone else.

The anatomy of a smile begins with people who care about one another, and it can be created most simply by a Purim costume and a feeling of love.

This story was adapted from Viewpoint, published by the National Council of Young Israel.

What We
Can Do

Virtual Tourists

Before a recent business/pleasure trip to Israel from my home in Chicago, I remembered an act of kindness I'd heard about last winter.

A Canadian woman about to go to Israel had asked friends in her small Jewish community to give her money to spend in Israel—not for "charity," but as payment for services to businesses in Israel.

Small businesses especially, and those catering to English-speaking tourists, are failing for lack of customers and moral support. She would be her community's "virtual tour guide." When she bought restaurant food, gifts, or other goods in Israel, she would pay double or triple the bill, explaining to the owners that this was "virtual support" from friends who couldn't come along to Israel but wanted to show solidarity.

Due in some part, I'm sure, to my fairly regular "Doses of Kindness" REMINDERS, instead of thinking of all the work and visits I had planned during my too-short five weeks in Israel, I, like you, said "Why not?" I quickly contacted some of my friends in Chicago to join together before my trip to do what the Canadian woman had done previously. This is the letter of thanks I sent after my trip to thank all of those who joined me for a "virtual tour" of Israel.

Friends,

I am just back from Israel, at times representing you, my generous Chicago friends. Thank you for your overwhelming support! Our forty-two "virtual" tourists spread $2500 among fifteen small struggling businesses in Israel, each of which, I felt, of-

fered something of real significance to its community.

One sum went to an elegant architecturally cutting-edge art center (a cooperative) near Allon Shvut—almost empty at 2 p.m.; several to businesses in the Old City and the Cardo in Jerusalem; and one to a shop at the Qumran Caves near the Dead Sea. A department manager there called me back to hug me. She made me tear up when she told me she was born at nearby Kibbutz Kalia, and that the older residents there tell her Israel has never felt so misunderstood and forsaken by the world since 1967. She said this would be a happy thing for them to hear.

One sum was to a stall-keeper in Machne Yehuda, the outdoor Jerusalem vegetable market repeatedly bombed; others to charming, empty "English speaking" restaurants; some to Ben Yehuda Street shops. One owner told me his shop had been totally destroyed by terrorists two years ago. "Was everyone here alright?" I asked. "Yes, thank God," he told me. Later, not from him, I learned that his wife had been seriously wounded, but miraculously survived. And, although I wouldn't take extra goods from owners (depleting stock wasn't the idea), he forced forty-two cards on me with the "Prayer for Travelers," which left us touched. Finally, Bob and I were lucky enough to serve home-baked cookies, juices, coffee and popcorn at a USO style "canteen" for soldiers serving in the Gush Etzion area, south of Bethlehem. We bought for you, through the volunteer/manager, special snacks for them.

What an experience. It exceeded my expectations for what a few people could very easily do to brighten lives in a land that's eternally important to all of us. I wish you were there!!!"

Bears from Bergenfield
By Claire Ginsburg Goldstein

I told my children that I thought it would be a great idea to have the kids I teach at our school make pins for children who are victims of terror in Israel. My son, Sam, who was almost eleven at the time, and a student at our school, thought it would be better to send teddy bears.

I mentioned Sam's idea to my class, and within a week we had our first donation, a "Build a Bear," from the "Build a Bear" teddy bear shop at a nearby mall.

After that first donation, I found a free way to advertise; a community leader taught me how to send emails to local email groups.

During the next several weeks the donations of stuffed toys started pouring in. I wondered, "How often would I be allowed to send emails to the same email lists?" "Who would help me spread the word?" "Would the newspapers publicize the project?" These were questions that were flooding my mind. I certainly hoped that I would find help.

It was not long before help arrived. I had heard about a woman named Sharon Evans, whose daughter, Monique, was wounded in a terrorist attack. Sharon had been speaking in my community about her new organization which was trying to provide financial support to families who are victims of terror.

A friend told me that Sharon was leaving soon for Israel. I called her and told her that we needed help bringing our bears to Israel and distributing them. She told me to meet her at JFK's King David lounge. I asked her if my daughter, Shira, could come and interview her daughter, Monique, who had barely survived a terrorist attack.

Shira helped me pack more than thirty bears into a duffel bag, along with our first donated "Build a Bear" We drove to JFK and spent an hour with Sharon and Monique. We discussed how we could get my family's project, "Bears from Bergenfield," off the ground.

As we handed over the "Build a Bear," we asked Sharon and Monique if they could hook us up with an organization that could distribute teddy bears to victims of terror. Sharon immediately made a call to Jerusalem to Yeshara Gold, the director of Kids for Kids. Yeshara told us to send the toys and her organization would distribute them to needy children.

We now give to fifteen hospitals and five organizations that assist victims of terror. Bears from Bergenfield has collected over 50,000 new and slightly used stuffed animals and teddy bears and we see no end in sight. We collect throughout the United States and hope to expand this venture to Canada and England and anywhere where people would like to join us.

Claire Ginsburg Goldstein's teaches seventh grade religious school class at Congregation Beth Israel of Bergenfield. Her class runs this program.

My Twelve-Year-Old Son's Appeal for a Poor Family in Israel

One *Sabbath* morning, my twelve-year-old son got up in front of the congregation in which he prays (sixth- thru eighth-graders with some of their parents) and made his own appeal for a poor family in Israel.

I was touched this Purim as my son raised over $180 for this family. I was moved not only by what he did, but that people, after giving their charity to the poor (a special Purim *mitzvah*) gave him more money to help him fulfill his goal.

Every time we stopped the car to deliver the Purim gift baskets of food he got out of the car and collected money for the poor family. I am proud of my community members in West Hempstead and especially proud of him to want to do this act of kindness for a needy family.

A Formula for Compassion

I was checking my emails and saw an email from an organization in Israel collecting for food for the hungry, which I instinctively deleted as junk mail. Then I read today's *Daily Dose of Kindness* about the mother who didn't have enough formula to feed her baby. I felt bad about it and then continued to read whatever other emails I had.

I went upstairs and started cooking chicken and chicken soup for Passover. As I was chopping the onions, I suddenly thought to myself, how callous I am, that here I am chopping onions for six chickens I am about to cook, and this mother doesn't have formula to feed her baby.

I stopped what I was doing, went back downstairs, back online, retrieved the food for the hungry email from the "trash bin," and made a donation.

Afterword

∽⫶⫶⫶⫶⫶∽

Mission Completed

My memories about the day that my wife Shoshana was killed are all a blur. The first thing I remember was our phone conversation at 5:30 in the morning, New York time. Shoshana spoke a mile a minute. She was so excited about being pregnant with our first child, about coming home in a few days and about being together with me again.

The next phone call came after I arrived at work. Shoshana's father called to tell me that there had been a bombing in a restaurant in Jerusalem. He explained that when Shoshana was in Israel she always called her parents immediately to reassure them whenever there was any type of incident—and that this time she had not called.

As soon as I got off the phone with my father-in-law, I called my rabbi. He told me to call him as soon as I found out conclusively one way or another.

There were phone calls throughout the day from my father-in-law telling me what friends and relatives had found out and finally the phone call from Shoshana's uncle who called to tell me that he had identified her body in the morgue. He kept on crying and could hardly utter a word.

As soon as I got off the phone with Shoshana's uncle, I called my rabbi. He told me to come straight to his house. By the time I arrived, my rabbi had already booked two tickets to Israel and made arrangements for a police escort to the airport. There didn't seem to be a car on the road anywhere during New York's afternoon rush hour as we sped from Brooklyn to Newark. We didn't even need the sirens or the flashing lights.

My rabbi sat by my side during the flight. I knew he had lost his father when he was a youngster and would understand what was going through my mind when I asked:

"Everyone has a mission. Did Shoshana finish her mission?"

He surprised me when he answered with only one word, "Yes."

"How do you know?" I queried.

"When a person dies, it means they have finished their mission," he replied.

His reply comforted me. That was the master plan. Shoshana's mission in this world had been completed. Although obviously, I would rather have had her back more than anything else, there was nothing I or anyone else could do to change things.

There is Good in Every Bad

During the traditional week of mourning, close to a thousand people came to comfort me. Hundreds of them were students, parents and friends whose lives were enriched by Shoshana in so many different ways. They told me how she had comforted them by telling them that "There is good in every bad." And so it is—in tragedy, there is opportunity to reach out to others and to turn something "bad" into something good and meaningful.

What pulls us through tragedies are the people who are there for us in our darkest hours—the friends and relatives who support us with our physical and emotional needs and the strangers who open their hearts to relieve our burdens. Here is the way a Jerusalem mother explains the situation.

ᴄ━✗✗✗✗━ᴄ

When Strangers Open Their Hearts

As the mother of a child who has undergone repeated hospitalizations, I can tell you firsthand how wonderful a medical clown can be, and not necessarily just for the patient.

Inevitably, parents of hospitalized children, having been given extra doses of help from above to somehow keep going when the situation is serious, start wilting just as the child starts feeling better. Just when the child wants to play, and the siblings want their mommy back, mommy has less than zero energy. Needless to say this is not a good situation.

One day I was sitting in a room visiting a colleague whose hospitalized child was, thank God, well on her way to recovery, as was my son, when in walked a medical clown. He took one look at the smiling toddler happily playing and the whistling grade school girl enjoying a workbook, and turned towards us. He saw two mothers, worn out and pale, with bags big enough to pack up a small household under our eyes. He started working on us and had us both in fits of laughter before he left.

That night when I came home for a few hours before my next shift, I suddenly had energy for my other children; time to "just talk" with my husband, instead of simply exchanging quick medical updates and urgent shopping lists. I could even relax on the couch for a bit before I went back.

Thank you, whoever you are. You may never realize how healing your clowning was, but I shall never forget.

Helping Others Helps Ourselves

"In every bad there is good." While the pain is sometimes so great that we don't know how we can carry on, it is exactly those feelings of pain that give us an extraordinary ability to help others in pain, as this woman from a community in the Shomron explains:

This month I enrolled in a course in medical clowning. We are a group of forty people of all different ages and backgrounds. It's an amazing opportunity to meet all kinds of people that ordinarily I would not get a chance to know.

The most inspiring thing about being in this group is that most of the people have had much pain and difficult trials in their lives, and have come to this course not only to develop the ability to face adversity with optimism and humor, but to help others find this ability within themselves as well. I feel privileged to be with these people.

We do a lot of exercises to help us become aware of our own emotions, the emotions of others, and the interaction between the two. The exercises are very silly and we spend a lot of time laughing!

What I have noticed is that all the laughter and silliness creates a lot of kindness. For instance, someone offered to bring food for the break. Now every week, several people bring food: salads, casseroles, homemade breads and cakes. People with cars offer rides to people who don't have cars.

The ability to clown stems from the meeting between happiness and sadness, so when someone suddenly encounters this meeting place, he or she is surrounded with love, support and hugs from others in the group. Once you receive this, you can give it to others.

We often try to escape from our deepest emotions of sadness, grief, disappointment and fear. When we can identify these feelings and acknowledge them in ourselves or others, we can turn them into something positive and creative.

What we are learning in medical clowning is first of all to get in touch with our own emotions and learn how they are expressed through our body language and facial expressions. When we learn this about ourselves, we can meet the patient where he is emotionally, and from there bring him to a happier feeling through clowning. In other words, you can't just pop into the room of a sick person in the hospital, wearing a funny get-up, and expect to cheer them up and get them to laugh. You have to know how to come into the room, how to introduce yourself, and most of all know how to connect with them where they are emotionally. There's your meeting place.

Many of the exercises are focused on copying the expression of someone else in the group, and then creating something of ourselves from that. This trains us to "listen," be sensitive, and honor where the other person is coming from in ways that are not necessarily verbal. We're currently on session five, and there are fifteen more to go. Somewhere in the midst of this process, each one of us will discover his or her own individual clown that exists inside of us—its character, its style, and the way that it expresses itself.

People who finish the course of twenty sessions go out to volunteer in hospital wards, senior citizen homes, and any other place where happiness can make a difference through helping people feel better about their lives. Dr. Patch Adams was the one who started this movement by opening a hospital in Virginia called "Gezundheit!" and spreading medical clowning throughout the world. You might be interested in looking at his website to learn more about medical clowning!

Do Something about It

The stories in this book are about people who see the opportunity to help others. And when they see that opportunity they grab it.

If you truly want to realize your greatest potential to help others, it's not enough to just read this book or to even help others once in a while. You need to surround yourself with people who are role models of kindness. If you do not see these types of people every day, you need to read about them, not just once, but all the time.

Read our emails, send us your stories and join us as a Partner in Kindness.

Wishing you blessings for all good things,
Shmuel Greenbaum

Glossary

Glossary

BAR MITZVAH: literally "person responsible for observance of *mitzvahs*"; refers to a Jewish boy on his thirteenth birthday, at which age he is considered an adult and responsible for his moral and religious duties. This milestone is often marked by a celebration which is also referred to as a *bar mitzvah*. (See MITZVAH).

BAT MITZVAH: literally "person responsible for observance of *mitzvahs*"; refers to a Jewish girl on her twelfth birthday, at which age she is considered an adult and responsible for her moral and religious duties. This milestone is often marked by a celebration which is also referred to as a *bat mitzvah*. (See MITZVAH).

BRIS: literally "covenant"; refers to *bris milah*—the circumcision ceremony, performed in accordance with the method prescribed by Jewish law.

CHALLAH: loaf of bread, often braided, eaten on the Sabbath, holidays, and other ceremonial occasions.

CHESED: kindness; also refers to the many types of kindness which are obligatory under Jewish law including: giving money to the poor, visiting the sick, burying the dead, welcoming guests to your home. (See www.TraditionOfKindness.org for more information).

HUMUS: Arabic term for chickpea; a popular Middle Eastern dip made from chickpeas, and spices.

KIDDUSH: literally "sanctification"; refers to blessings made over a cup of wine during Sabbath and holiday meals. Also refers to a social gathering with refreshments held after Sabbath and holiday morning services, which begins with the blessings made over a cup of wine.

LEBEN: yogurt.

MEGILLAT ESTHER: the Biblical *Book of Esther.*

MENTSCH: Yiddish term for a decent, upright person.

MATZAH: flat brittle bread made exclusively from flour and water; traditionally eaten during the Passover holiday.

MITZVAH: commandment or religious obligation; commonly used to mean a good deed of any kind. See also BAR MITZVAH and BAT MITVAH.

MORDECHAI HAYEHUDI: Mordechai the Jew. Hero in the Biblical story of Esther. Cousin of Queen Esther. (See PURIM).

PURIM: Holiday which dates back to 356 BCE. The origins and customs of the holiday are found in the Biblical *Book of Esther.*

REBBE: teacher of *Torah.*

ROSH HASHANAH: Biblical holiday which occurs in the fall; the Jewish New Year; also known as the "Day of Judgment."

SEDER: A ceremonial dinner a ceremonial dinner incorporating a liturgy of the exodus of the Jews from Egypt, celebrated on the first night of Passover in Israel and on both the first and second nights outside of Israel.

SHABBOS: The Sabbath; observed from sundown on Friday afternoon until nightfall on Saturday evening.

SHALOM ZACHOR: Celebration held the first Friday night after a baby boy is born; light refreshments are served.

SHEVA BRACHOS: seven blessings recited at Jewish weddings; also refers to festive meals held in honor of the bride and groom during the week following the wedding.

SHOFAR: Ram's horn blown on Rosh Hashanah and Yom Kippur.

TORAH: 1. Law or instruction; 2. First five books of the Bible; 3. Hand-written scroll of parchment which is read during prayer services and contains the first five books of the Bible; 4. Entire body of Jewish law and sacred writings including the oral tradition contained in the *Talmud*.

UPSHERN: a Yiddish term literally meaning to shear or cut off; there is an ancient tradition of not cutting the hair of a boy until his third birthday, a minor ceremony and celebration has grown around it with the honor of cutting usually given to a rabbi and often shared by several people; in Israel many children are taken to Meron on *Lag B'Omer* for the *upshern*.

YARMULKES: Yiddish word for head coverings; derived from the Aramaic, *"yira malka,"* which means "fear of the King."

YESHIVA: Hebrew term; literally "sitting down." An institution for the study of *Torah*.

Kindness Organizations in Israel

◇ Bikes for Kids - rjr@013.net

◇ The Chicken Lady - www.aish.com/jewishissues/
jewishsociety/the_chicken_lady.asp

◇ Ezer Mizion - www.ezer-mizion.org.il

◇ The Gush Etzion Foundation -
www.gush-etzion.org.il/foundation.asp

◇ IMACHDUT - margotg@bezeqint.net

◇ KIDS FOR KIDS - www.kidsforkids.net

◇ Lema'an Achai - www.lemaanachai.org

◇ Neshoma Tehorah - neshomatehora@Safemail.net

◇ Raise Your Spirits - alizahh@hotmail.com.

◇ Table to Table - www.tabletotable.org.il

◇ The Telegemach - c/o Avraham Ellis, Lubavitch 11/3,
Betar Eilit, 99879 Israel
Telephone: 011-972-8-941-2337 Fax: 011-972-8-941-1907

◇ Yad Sarah - www.yadsarah.org

◇ Yad Gedaliah - yadgedaliah@yahoo.com

◇ Zichron Menachem - www.zichronmenachem.org

Sponsor
Dedications

With Love in Memory of
Levi Yitzchak Olenick

Levi loved people – his greatest pleasure was to be of "service" to others and his enthusiasm was unusual... This extended to being a dedicated doctor and an energetic participant of his community on many levels. He was inspired by different kinds of people but was extremely fair minded, not easily impressed by wealth or fame... To live by ethics and morals was his "wealth" and he invested his entire life to this goal. As a responsible and thoughtful husband, a caring and encouraging father, a loyal son and son-in-law, a helpful brother with a listening heart, and a playful uncle. He accomplished so much in life and his unique qualities will always be remembered...

Rivka, Yoni and Alexander Olenick • Loving mom and dad Ruth and Elliott Olenick • Chana, Phil, Itiel, Tammy, Rinat Olenick • Michal, Moishe, Batsheva and Perri Goldfein • Irving and Florence Posner • Shmuel Greenbaum

In memory of a very special brother,
Levi Yitzchak Olenick,
a true confidant in every way; you are truly missed.
Ellen, Yecheskel, Chaya Raizel and Avrohom Medetsky

To My Brother,
Larry,
I'll always remember the little boy whose smile could light up a room and who put his whole being into everything he did. You never gave up. We miss you. Love Fran, Steve & Jesse Adelson

In loving memory of
Shoshana,
*whose presence was woven into the fabric of our family
from the very beginning.*

*Pinchas and Shoshana, Natan, Alex, Elana, Elisheva,
Shalom, Chaim and families*

In memory of
Shoshana Greenbaum
by Eliyahu Dovid and Shifra Hayman

In memory of Shoshana Hayman Greenbaum

In Memory of HALB's
Morah Shoshana
— Julie and Shabsi Schreier, Woodmere, NY

In memory of
Shoshana,
whose memory is a blessing to all.
— Louis and Elke Chapman

In memory of
Morah Shoshana (Hayman) Greenbaum
From the Hasson Family

In loving memory of our niece,
Ellie
adored daughter of Haviva and Joe Zelinger.
Elie & Hindy Lederman, Ra'anana, Israel

Dedicated in memory of my dear friend
BatSheva Unterman,
whose last act in this world
was to save her baby daughter while under a terrorist attack.
Her selflessness in death
exemplified a life lived fulfilling acts of kindness.

In honor of
Edward Solomon *z"l*, **Adam Kagan, Dima and Ana Govorko,**
Eliecer Saldarriaga, Mulu Tesema, Ana Suarez, Valerie Linabury
and **Sima Mamroud**
for all their kind acts over the years.

In Memory of
Neil S. Lieblich, *M.D.*
May 2, 1954 - June 23, 2008
Kindly, Brilliant and Beloved
May He Eternally Rest in Peace

To my wonderful mother,
Barbara Levitan Sexter,
model caregiver,
pure heart & soul.
Donna Karmel, Los Angeles, CA

To my endlessly kind husband,
Andy Gross,
Happy 60th Birthday
and many more!

In memory –
Batya bat Yitzchak
Loved by all who knew her.

Debi and Howard Reece
Passaic, NJ USA

Aviva & Nate Lichtenstein —
In memory of Henry Lichtenstein
& Dr. Nahum Zackai

Martin and Audrey Greenbaum
Mazel tov and best wishes Shmuel

Doris & Wilbur Jaffe, SD/CA
Continued successful endeavors

Shmuel —
Your kindness inspires ours! The
world is a better place as a result!

In honor of our mom and bubby —
Fay Berg
All our love, the Shulman Family

In loving memory of my father —
Shlomo
ben Moshe and Miryam Linzer

For Avigail, Miriam, and Natan
May you only know kindness.

In honor of S. Greenbaum,
A true hero and role model.

Mira Nakash, Belle Harbor —
To the devoted women of our
Wednesday prayer group.

In honor of our parents —
Neil and Toby Fischer
and **Harriet Moskowitz**
for their acts of kindness.

Jack Mathis, Laguna Niguel, CA —
Kindness is the practice
of the religion of Love.

In Memory of Yoel Aron Montal
– Bracha Banash

Yisroel – You inspire me. Love JH

"Love. Peace. Redemption." – SP

Cathy Sherman – www.devardoc.com

The Bukiets, West Orange, NJ

Barbara Michael, Columbia, MO

Ron and Marsha Weiskopf

"With Gratitude": The Ausubels

The Gruenfeld Family, Woodmere,NY

Mazel Tov Naomi Weiss on graduating
from SKA 2009

Danielle Grushko, Jerusalem, Israel

In memory of the Holtzbergs

In memory of Alte Brucha Miriam

Mazal Zirkind & Family

Miriam & Carl Singer and Family

Simon Shamoun, NY

In memory – Rabbi M. Lonner *z"l*

The Stareshefsky Family

Shmuel, thanks for heightening our
awareness!

More About
Partners in Kindness

Partners in Kindness
Worldwide Speaking Tour

After Shmuel Greenbaum's wife was killed by a suicide bomber in a Jerusalem restaurant, he responded to his tragedy not with hatred and anger, but by teaching the world kindness through the personal stories of every day people. His two websites send kindness e-mails to thousands of subscribers directly and are reprinted in hundreds of publications, which reach millions of readers.

Shmuel is fascinating audiences from Larnaca, Cyprus to London, England with a dynamic presentation. Rather than focusing on hatred and anger, Shmuel focuses on the positive. Through stories and audience participation, Shmuel plays up the emotions of the crowd and rivets his audience's attention. Participants come away feeling very positive and excited about doing something great.

For more information, contact us at:
info@PartnersInKindness.org

Audience Responses

This past summer, I had a family emergency. My cousin, who was only 23 years old and one of my best friends, was murdered in Israel. It was very hard for me because I was close to him and I have not seen him for four years when this happened. He was a very young guy, a very beautiful person, inside and out.

After the tragedy, I found myself not being the same anymore. I did not want to go out with friends or do anything. I found myself being more distant with people because I thought that I could not trust anyone after what happened to my cousin. I kept thinking about how people could be so cruel and selfish and just so inhuman and often wondered if there are many, if any, nice and wonderful people left in this world.

After listening to Mr. Greenbaum, I, first of all, was much moved and second of all, his story about kindness and his project about kindness and teaching it to others restored my thoughts. Thank you very much for having him come in. he was absolutely great. Definitely have him come back next semester if possible.

Loyola University, Chicago, Illinois

You came to my high school, Wauwatosa West and I just wanted to say thanks for being inspiring! I was amazed at your personal strength in dealing with tragedy by having a positive impact, and I signed up for the weekly emails so I can (hopefully) go through life constructively, and spread kindness.

Thanks again for coming!

Wauwatosa West High School, Wauwatosa, Wisconsin

◇ ◇ ◇

Thirteen months ago, my mother was involved in a hit and run accident while crossing the street. Fortunately, my mom suffered only a bruise on her right leg. The first few minutes when I received the news, however, I was uncertain of the outcome. Therefore, I cursed God and the man who hit my mother, with enough rage to kill him if I received the chance.

Today, I could say that if a member of my family or if a close friend were to be murdered, I would seek revenge through violence or at least, displaced anger. I cannot fathom anyone else would think differently. A few days ago, Shmuel Greenbaum proved me wrong.

Mr. Greenbaum was a guest speaker whose wife was murdered by a suicide bomber. Instead of anger, he responded with kindness. His story truly produces astonishment for anyone who hears it.

Stuyvesant High School, New York, New York

◇   ◇   ◇

It is sad to look around and understand that so much of our world is defined by hate. As an idealist who has faith in the common person, this observation is especially affecting. But it is inspirational, if nothing else, to see that every so often there are people who try and fight this dreary system that we are born into. A movement such as the one Mr. Greenbaum advocates serves a reminder that we are at least capable, if unwilling, to do kindness.

I walked into Lecture Hall A today, expecting to attend the lecture given by Shmuel Greenbaum for one period. I ended up staying for four. What I saw today was stirring for a number of reasons, and was a great example of the type of intellectual discussion that our school can boast. I also found our guest speaker, Shmuel Greenbaum, to be captivating for several reasons.

Shmuel Greenbaum is an extraordinary human being. The tragedy that he was forced to endure is something that none of us should ever have to be exposed to. And to have to deal with the horrors of September the 11th, a mere 32 days later? Now that defines tragedy in a person's life.

I don't think that many people exist who could respond to an experience like that with anything but hatred and rage. Greenbaum reacted, instead, with kindness. It is an act, that is equally beautiful as it is hopeful for the future.

Listening to that man speak, your heart lifts. Hearing of all the good that he has put into the world, in the wake of such a horrible catastrophe, you cannot help but adore him. If only more people could live their days out like this man, you think to yourself, if only everyone else could practice kindness in the way that Shmuel Greenbaum has, the world would truly be a better place. It is for this reason, that I deeply admire Mr. Greenbaum, and strongly feel that he is the most commendable person that we have observed thus far in this class.

When it comes down to it, there is no denying the fact that Shmuel Greenbaum is an amazing individual, who is truly dedicating his life to making the world a better place. It is so uplifting, so enlightening, so refreshing to hear someone like him talk to simply bubble over with excitement at the thought of doing good in the world. He is in his way, a role model to us all.

Let me say this. When his compassion campaign hits the New York Subways, I will be one of its most enthusiastic fans.

Stuyvesant High School, New York, New York

Sponsor

Sponsor Partners in Kindness programs, e-mails, radio shows, and upcoming books.

For more information, contact us at:
info@PartnersInKindness.org

Volunteer

Partners in Kindness can always use volunteers. Some of the skills we need are:

- ◇ *Editing*
- ◇ *Photography and Graphic Design*
- ◇ *Public Relations and Marketing*
- ◇ *Acting*
- ◇ *Radio / TV Production*
- ◇ *Web Development*
- ◇ *Clerical Work*

If you would like to help, please e-mail your résumé and/or a description of how you can help to:
info@PartnersInKindness.org